IS THERE A DOCTOR IN THE HOUSE?

IS THERE A DOCTOR IN THE HOUSE?

AN INSIDER'S STORY AND ADVICE ON
BECOMING A BIBLE SCHOLAR

BEN WITHERINGTON III

ZONDERVAN®

ZONDERVAN.com/
AUTHORTRACKER
follow your favorite authors

ZONDERVAN

Is There a Doctor in the House?
Copyright © 2011 by Ben Witherington III

This title is also available as a Zondervan ebook. Visit www.zondervan.com/ebooks.

This title is also available in a Zondervan audio edition. Visit www.zondervan.fm.

Requests for information should be addressed to:

Zondervan, *Grand Rapids, Michigan 49530*

Library of Congress Cataloging-in-Publication Data
    Witherington, Ben III.
       Is there a doctor in the house? : an insider's story and advice on becoming a
    Bible scholar / Ben Witherington III.
       p. cm.
    ISBN 978-0-310-49302-0 (softcover)
      1. Bible — Study and teaching. 2. Theology--Study and teaching. I. Title.
    BS600.3.W58 2011
    220.071'1 — dc22
                                         2011007545

Cover design: Chris Tobias
Interior design: Cindy LaBreacht

Printed in the United States of America

11 12 13 14 15 16 /DCI/ 20 19 18 17 16 15 14 13 12 11 10 9 8 7 6 5 4 3 2 1

To AFTE and to the John Wesley Fellows—

both those who are already doctors

and those who are doctors in training

CONTENTS

THE ILLUSTRATED
GUIDE TO A PHD[1]

Imagine a circle that contains all of human knowledge:

By the time you finish elementary school,
you know a little:

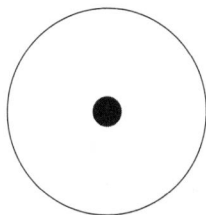

By the time you finish high school, you know a bit more:

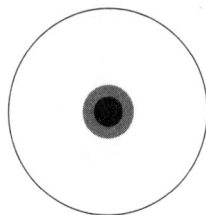

---

1. *The Illustrated Guide to a PhD* was created by Matt Might and may be found on his website: http://matt.might.net/articles/phd-school-in-pictures/. Used by permission.

With a bachelor's degree, you gain a specialty:

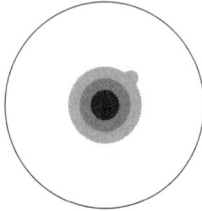

A master's degree deepens that specialty:

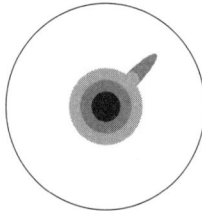

Reading research papers takes you
to the edge of human knowledge:

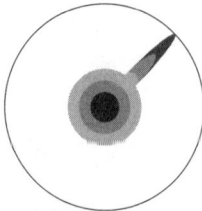

Once you're at the boundary, you focus:

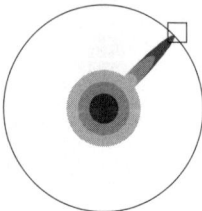

You push at the boundary for a few years:

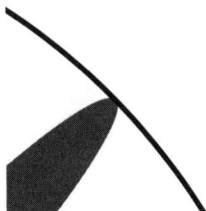

Until one day, the boundary gives way:

And, that dent you've made is called a PhD:

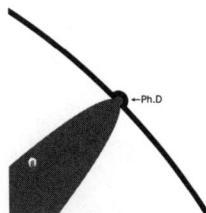

←Ph.D

Of course, the world looks different to you now:

So, don't forget the bigger picture:

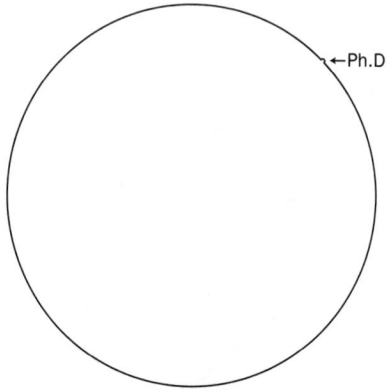

←Ph.D

Keep pushing.

FAST FORWARD

I was late for my connecting flight in St. Louis. So late, in fact, that I was running through the concourse like a man with his hair on fire. I was on my way to Seattle to give lectures at Seattle Pacific University, and almost as soon as I got off the plane, I expected to be met by some university dignitary at the airport, or so I had been told.

The sweat had begun to pour off me the faster I ran, tugging along my roller bag, with my boarding pass clutched in the other hand. I slowed down when I got to the gate only to discover they had moved the gate five doors down, so I was back running again. I could see the gate agent closing the door, and I started hollering, "Don't close the door; please, don't close the door"; but she was oblivious to my plight. If I didn't make this flight, there wasn't another one for hours and hours, and I would miss several of the lectures and the main address I was supposed to give to a considerable crowd of people. Snagging the gate agent just before she left, I begged her to let me run down the concourse to the plane, which she reluctantly agreed to, calling ahead to tell them not to pull the plane back from the gate yet.

As I reached the end of the seemingly endless tunnel leading to the plane, completely soaked in sweat, I saw that there was a small gap between the end of the tunnel and the beginning of the plane. Just when I got to that gap, my boarding pass slipped out of my sweaty palm and fell through that narrow gap onto the tarmac below. Instinctively I lurched to grab the ticket as it fell, completely splitting the backside of my new trousers! There was a man on the tarmac below who gently handed me up my ticket through the gap as I was busily pulling my dress shirt out of my pants to cover my mishap. The stewardess standing in the door had witnessed this entire debacle and was snickering, and I could hardly blame her.

As I slid into my seat, my mind could not decide whether I was more relieved to be on the plane, or more panicked about the fact that some major factotum of the university was supposed to meet me at the airport. If America were still an honor and shame culture, I suppose I would have had to refuse the honor of lecturing, since I didn't have another suit with me, but hey, I was heading to Seattle—the home of casual dress and Starbucks coffee. I figured I would survive one way or another.

As I came off the plane in Seattle some hours later, there at the gate was a man in blue jeans and a lumberjack shirt. It was my old friend and editor Dan Reid, not the president of Seattle-Pacific. I exclaimed, "Thank you, Jesus, for sending me someone that looks even worse than I do!" Just another day in the life of a Bible scholar who was trained to believe "the world is your parish."

This little book is perhaps my most personal, so in it there will be more sharing of my own experiences along the way, and a bit more sharing from the heart, including sharing some of my poetry. Sometimes the process of becoming a Bible scholar is so demanding and even mind-numbing that I found I needed an artistic outlet to express what I was thinking about it in a nonacademic, non-cut-and-dried way. For me the vehicle that expresses the sound of my soul, or the right side of my brain at least, is poetry.

Becoming a Bible scholar is, of course, different for each person, and in each case it is a deeply personal journey that will test your metal, plumb the depths of your soul, and show you just how much willpower you have to climb up the necessary mountains. With that in mind, I am offering a few poems, judicially chosen and placed at the end of the chapters, for reflection. They are also intended to tease your minds into active thought in a different way about the subject matter of the book. They reflect my life motto, borrowed from Anselm: *fides quaerens intellectum* ("faith seeking understanding")—and since I am a writer, "faith seeking self-expression." Here is a little food for thought about a life in motion and commotion.

THE MAZE

VOICE ONE—
THE CONSCIENCE

You don't get there sooner
Running faster in that direction,
It only ruins your temper
Your color and complexion.

VOICE TWO—
THE EMOTIONS

If you can't remember
Whether you've been here before
I fear you'll never find
The exit or the door.

VOICE THREE—
THE WILL

You grow weary of the game
You grow wary of the claim
Cause all paths look the same,
And no one is to blame.

VOICE FOUR—
THE MIND

Did you take the trouble
To think the path through,
Before you even started,
Before you turned blue?

VOICE ONE—
THE CONSCIENCE

Are you going round in circles,
Retracing your selections,
Has it occurred to you,
To ask for directions?

VOICE TWO—
THE EMOTIONS

Every turn you take,
Every move you make,
Every path you forsake,
Could be a mistake.

VOICE THREE—
THE WILL

Some are not phased
By a complex maze,
It doesn't take days,
Or leave you amazed.

VOICE FOUR—
THE MIND

Seeing the end from the beginning,
Shows you which way to go,
If only you'd had the foresight,
To start off quite slow.

VOICE TWO—
THE EMOTIONS

And now it's getting dark,
And all the noises gone,
Should I just stop and rest,
Or should I be moving on?

THE STILL SMALL VOICE

"My Word is a lamp unto your feet,
And a light unto your path."

BW III
July 17, 2007

1

IN PRINCIPIO ERAT VERBUM:
PRELIMINARY CONSIDERATIONS

First Things

The students were sitting everywhere imaginable. In the seats, in the aisles, in the huge windows that were open, even in chairs on the platform, from which Dr. Boyd was teaching in old Saunders Hall. We must have been violating the fire code in forty different ways, but it didn't seem to matter. Everyone was riveted by the lectures of Dr. Bernard Boyd, who on this day in 1972 was holding forth on Old Testament history, intermingled with quotes from Shakespeare, anecdotes from his time as a chaplain during World War II, and the occasional buttonholing of this or that student on some topic du jour. We were in the middle of the winter of our discontent over the Vietnam War, and yet somehow this professor had us all excited about studying the Bible and learning it well, studying it in its historical, archaeological, literary, theological, social, and cultural contexts.

For me these were formative years, not only because I came to embrace fully the Christian faith and make it my own during my time at the University of North Carolina, but also because I began to have an inkling of what God would want me to do with my life. It has been said you become what you admire, and I suppose that old adage has proved true in my life. I admired no teacher more than the James A. Gray professor of Bible at Carolina—Bernie Boyd. And I was not alone. It has been estimated that several thousand of us went into some kind of ministry, including the ministry of Bible teaching and scholarship, because of him, despite the stern admonition of St. James that "not many of you should become teachers" (James 3:1).

Let me be clear that Dr. Boyd had not suggested or even hinted it would be easy to become a real Bible teacher, much less a Bible scholar. After all, as he said, it required an exacting knowledge of the biblical languages (Greek, Hebrew, and Aramaic), not to mention the languages in which Bible scholarship was mostly done (English, French, and German). It required a love for history and archaeology and things arcane. It required a love for literature, literary genres, and a certain literary sensitivity. It required an understanding of theology, and ethics, and ancient religions and philosophies. You had to have a working knowledge in a plethora of fields just to have the background to be able to deal with a book as rich and complex as the Bible.

Dr. Boyd made it evident from the outset: to be a Bible teacher, much less a Bible scholar, was a daunting task, and the faint of heart and the unmotivated and undisciplined should just abandon ship before the ship even sailed. As the British would say, you had to be polymath to be a Bible expert. No doubt about it. Although there are levels of expertise in various subdisciplines of biblical studies to be had and cultivated, in one sense every Bible teacher has to be a G.P., a General Practitioner, just to be able to get to the point of focusing on one particular dimension of the Bible and its literature. The foundation on which any Bible teacher or scholar stands must necessarily be broad and well-built to bear the weight of whatever special construction one might wish to build on top of it.

For me, what crystallized during those many hours and days of sitting under the tutelage of Bernard Boyd was not merely a love for the Bible and its teaching and teachings, but a dawning realization that my love for languages, for history, for literature, for the Latin and Greek classics, for Western culture—in short, my love for all those subjects I was most keen about—could all be furthered and further developed if I became a Bible teacher and Bible scholar. The Bible entailed all those subjects, and much more. I didn't have to choose between a love for languages or a love for history or a love for literature or a love for theology or philosophy as a career, if I chose to pursue a career in learning and teaching and writing about the Bible. For me, it was one-stop shopping. All the things that God had given me some ability to study and learn, and a joy in doing so, were the very prerequisites I needed to be a good Bible student, then teacher, then scholar.

What about my love for and degree in English literature? Beside the fact that the KJV is the greatest work ever in English literature, it is also the most influential piece of English literature on the great masters of our language—writers like Shakespeare and Milton, and Herbert and Donne, and so many more. I discovered that to focus on the Bible didn't mean I had to give up English literature. It meant I had to focus on certain kinds of English literature—for example, English Bible versions and translations. But is all this study and language preparation really necessary to be a good Bible teacher or scholar?

Educated Fool or Fool for Christ?

Because so many people tend to think that the Bible belongs to everyone and everyone can interpret it—which, of course, in one sense is true (it is, after all, the people's Book)—there is a tendency to think that a person can become a Bible expert just by rolling up one's sleeves and studying some English translation of the Bible. "The B-I-B-L-E, yes, that's the book for me"—plus nothing, seems to be the assumption in some quarters.

I remember the advice some folks gave me before I went off to Carolina and then later to seminary: "Don't be so open-minded your brains fall out." Of course, I understand that warning—the Christian pilgrimage should not become something that could be called Gullible's Travels. Ideas have consequences, and they are seldom neutral. You shouldn't believe everything you are taught, even if you are taught it by your favorite professor.

The essence of the advice I was given was not to become so educated that you lose your religion. It is true that some people have lost their religion in the process of seriously studying the Bible. This sad fact has caused an overreaction in some cases. There is an anti-intellectual bent to some forms of conservative Christianity, and I ran into that before, during, and after my process of higher education.

Some years ago I had a student come up to me after a seminary class at Asbury who said, "I don't know why I need to learn all this stuff you are teaching me. I know my Bible and I can just get up into the pulpit and the Spirit will give me utterance."

I replied, "Yes, Billy, you can do that, but it is a shame you are not giving the Spirit more to work with."[2] Beware of using the Holy Spirit as a labor-saving device!

Billy's approach will never do if one wants really to know and understand the Bible. Profound contextual study of the Bible is necessary for such understanding. As I like to put it, a text without a context is just a pretext for whatever you want it to mean.

The Difference between a Student, a Teacher, and a Scholar

At the outset of this book, it would be good to make some distinctions. One can become a serious student of the Bible without becoming a teacher of the Bible, and one can become an excellent teacher of the Bible without becoming a well-published Bible scholar. This book is about all three of these things, but the focus of this book is on what it takes to become a good and even well-published Bible scholar.

There are many excellent teachers of the Bible who know their field well but hardly ever publish. Bernard Boyd was one such person. This in no way meant he wasn't a scholar. It just meant he wasn't a *well-published* scholar. In fact, decades ago he did some remarkable archaeological work in Israel and helped discover one of the first horned altars there.

I would say, however, that to be a truly good teacher of the Bible at a college or seminary level, one does need to aspire to be a scholar of the Bible. You need to know your field. You have to boil it up before you can boil it down for your students. The bar is set higher for those professions. If, however, your goal is simply to be a good Bible study leader, Sunday school teacher, or Christian high school teacher of the Bible, at a minimum you must be a serious student of the Bible and read good biblical scholarship as you prepare your

---

2. N.B. One of my best friends in the guild of biblical scholars, A. J. Levine, tells me she also had almost exactly the same experience with a student at Vanderbilt and gave him in essence the same response. I take some comfort knowing I am not alone in getting exasperated with the anti-intellectualism of some conservative Christian students of the Bible.

lessons and Bible studies. We must all "study to find ourselves approved," as the Good Book says (cf. 2 Tim. 2:15 KJV).

In other words, to be a serious student, much less a teacher or scholar of the Bible, you must have a love for learning—and not just learning during a particular period of your life, but lifelong learning. At the outset of my journey toward becoming a biblical scholar, I realized that this huge undertaking would require much more than just a commitment to some intensive years of education. I would have to follow Johannes Bengel's dictum: "Apply the whole of yourself to the text, apply the whole of the text to yourself." It has been said that the hammer shapes the hand, but I say the Bible shapes the man or woman who picks it up and tries to learn it. The Bible has done far more to and for me than I have ever done for it.

It's still a work in progress for me, as it is for any other serious student, teacher, or scholar of the Bible. The work is never finished, and our knowledge is only partial, even at the end of one's life. Consider this book an invitation to strive to become an expert student or teacher or scholar of the Bible. It is a noble if daunting task, and in the subsequent chapters we will deal with the various aspects of what it takes to become a real Bible scholar.

A Revelation in the Mountains

It was the summer of 1969, after Woodstock and after Neil Armstrong had walked on the moon. I was a high school student with a driver's license and a love for adventure, potentially a volatile combination. I had borrowed my father's 1955 Chevy two-tone Bel Air—column shift, and more metal in it than a Patton tank. My friend Doug Harris and I had slipped off up to the mountains on the weekend, to joy ride on the Blue Ridge Parkway. All of a sudden, something untoward and unexpected happened. The clutch blew out on the car, and as the Bible says, "My countenance fell." I knew there were no gas stations and no help to be found on the Blue Ridge Parkway, so we ended up pushing the car off the Parkway and down into a Texaco station. We were stranded—stranded, that is, until we realized we could stick out our thumbs and hitchhike back to High Point, North Carolina, where we lived.

The first persons to give us a ride were an elderly mountain couple dressed in black and driving an old black car—a Plymouth, if memory serves. As we began to ride down the road with these senior citizens, Doug, now a lawyer in North Carolina, decided to strike up a conversation. His opening gambit was, "What did you think about Neil Armstrong's walk on the moon, and all those beautiful pictures of the beautiful blue sphere of the world revolving in space?" The answer he got stunned even Doug....

"That was all fake. Just a TV stunt. Any sensible person knows the world is not round and revolving," declared the man driving the car.

Doug, who did not recognize invincible ignorance when he saw it, was prone to argue (doubtless it is why he later became a lawyer). He retorted, "Why in the world would you say that?" asked Doug. As for me, I was whispering to Doug in the back seat, "Hush up. We need this ride."

The answer was definitive: "It says in the book of Revelations that the angels will stand on the four corners of the world. Couldn't be round if it has four corners, now could it?" said the elderly driver. We had been picked up by some of the last remaining Flatlanders in Appalachia. Beware of anyone who begins a sentence, "It says in the book of Revelations [plural]." That is not the exact title of the last book of the Bible. The man's reason for saying the world was not revolving was explained in a rhetorical question he asked Doug, "Have you ever walked out of your house at night and been standing upside down? I don't think so!" the man snorted.

Now what was wrong with this student of the Bible? It wasn't his piety, nor was it his knowledge of what the Bible says at one juncture in Revelation. It was that he read the Bible anachronistically and just assumed that the Bible was teaching cosmology in addition to theology, when in fact saying that "the angels will go to the four corners or come from the four corners of the earth" is no more than saying they will come from or go to all the major points on the compass. The passage wasn't trying to teach the shape of the earth at all!

It was precisely experiences like this growing up in the Old South that led me to realize two things: (1) the Bible is the most widely known, misunderstood, and misinterpreted book on the planet, and (2) it would take everything I could muster to do the

Bible justice and help correct a lot of the misconceptions and misreadings of the Bible. What follows in this book is something of a how-to guide to becoming a budding Bible scholar, because frankly, in an age of growing biblical illiteracy, we need more of them or else we may expect more encounters like the one I had on that hot day in the mountains of North Carolina. That encounter demonstrated to me beyond cavil that a little knowledge of the Bible could be a dangerous thing. Ignorance is not bliss when it comes to the truth of and about God's Word. Indeed, ignorance is the enemy of the truth. The only question is whether or not one can handle the truth about the Bible and keep listening to its voice.

DISRUPTIVE GRACE

Shattering the smattering
Of calm I had created
Grace, a gratuity
Disrupted my day.

Interrupting the ennui
I kept on feeling
An alien intruder
Stepped in my way.

Pacifying the pestering
Voice that kept nagging
I sought out a sanctuary
Any port in a storm.

Reluctantly resigned
To divine solicitation
The carols and bells
Beguiled me again.

Unbidden, unwanted
Joy overcame me
In spite of reluctance
Immersed once more.

Profoundly pregnant
Stuffed with the sacred
I wondered as I wandered
Out the back door.

Who sent out the signal
That lured and allured me
Called me and caught me
On that cold day?

A Father frantically calling?
A Son prodigally prodding?
A Spirited homing device?
GPS grace?

Or was it the familiar
Plaintive lament
Of a newborn child
Who was Heaven sent?

Some calls must be answered
Some cries must be heard
Some voices are insistent,
Especially the Word's.

BW III, 2007

2

SEEK AND YE SHALL FIND:
CHOOSING A SCHOOL, A PROGRAM, A MENTOR

Finding the Good Doctor

It is trite but true that we are all, to one extent or another, a product of our education. Suppose that you have already had a good undergraduate education and indeed have finished master's level work in "divinity" or biblical studies. This may in some cases be sufficient for you to be a teacher of the Bible in some parts in the world, but not in others. It may well be more than plenty to prepare you to be a good Sunday school teacher or preacher of God's Word. I do, however, grow weary of ministers who say, "I'm no expert in the Bible," but then they go out and preach it or teach it every week! Ask yourself this question: Would you go to a dentist who says, "I'm no expert in drilling but heck, let's start with you?" I don't think so.

It is a high and noble calling to be a teacher or minister of the Word, and you don't have to have a PhD to do so. But you must have a deep and wide knowledge of the Bible and a commitment always to study and use the best commentaries and resources you can find to understand the Bible better and to prepare your lessons and sermons. A teacher's or minister's library is one of his or her most vital tools of the trade.

Let's suppose, however, that a terminal degree—which is to say, a doctoral degree—is indeed required for you to teach the Bible in the context where you operate and to which you are called. This obviously means you will have to pursue that degree. Choosing a school, a mentor, and a program becomes crucial, and to some extent your choices will depend on your previous education and how well you did or did not do.

I never enjoy telling people they don't have good enough grades to do doctoral work in a good doctoral program, but I am doing them no good if I am not honest with them. Sometimes, however, the truth about oneself is heartbreaking. But it is better to find out in advance of undertaking the rigors of doctoral work, if possible, whether or not one is cut out for that sort of program. This is better than to have moved, spent a ton of money, taken comprehensive exams, asked your spouse to make huge sacrifices, and then failed to even get into the dissertation phase of doctoral work. Even more heartbreaking is to fail when you have rounded the last bend on the track, and then are derailed because the dissertation is found wanting.

Let's say, however, that you have the education, the training, the inclination, the intelligence, and the calling to do doctoral work in biblical studies. How do you decide where to go? For the North American student, there are two rather different choices. One choice is to stay in this country and get a North American style PhD. This generally takes five to seven years and costs upward of $100,000 (counting all expenses, some of which grants or scholarships from the school will cover).

This course of action will involve: (1) a number of required courses, (2) comprehensive exams, and (3) finally, if you are not brain dead yet, the dissertation, capped off with its examination by the faculty. My motto when doing my thesis was, finish the dissertation before it finishes you. It is a truth that doctoral dissertations will test your metal, and you will find out what sort of stuff you are made of.

Here's a truth about doctoral programs that many do not know — despite their high cost, they do not make money for the institution in question. In fact, in many cases they are loss leaders, because they are enormously labor intensive for an American doctoral faculty. This is why some schools admit so few doctoral students into a program in a given year, which makes the competition for places all the more fierce. I know of schools where, if you have not made a perfect or nearly perfect score on the GRE (Graduate Record Exam) or the relevant parts of the GRE and any other such tests, you will not even be considered for admission.

Study Abroad

There is, however, another option than studying in the U.S., namely, doing a PhD in the British system. What's the difference between an American and a British PhD? In 2010 there is less difference than there used to be, as some British institutions do now require course work and some exams prior to dissertating. They may even require a preliminary ThM degree, as is the case in some American schools. But by and large, the British system largely involves just a mentored dissertation. It can take three to five years to accomplish this, and in fact it costs less than in the U.S., especially if you finish the degree in less time than would be likely in America.

Here is where I tell you my story. I certainly could have done my doctoral work in the U.S. In fact, at one point Bruce Metzger at Princeton asked me if I would be interested in doing a doctoral dissertation under him at Princeton. When he suggested he would like me to do something on an obscure church father named Didymus the Blind, I politely declined. What I wanted to do was a dissertation on a red-hot topic of the day—women and their roles in the NT. Furthermore, I knew even in 1977 that I could finish much more quickly in the British system, and since my scholarship from A Foundation for Theological Education (AFTE) would only cover three years, the better part of valor was to study abroad. I felt I had had enough course work anyway, except in German, which I intended to take as soon as I began my doctoral work.

So I applied to both Oxford and Durham to do a DPhil and was accepted at both schools. I had asked about studying with J. N. D. Kelly at Oxford, but he was in fact nearing retirement, and so I was offered a chance to work with George B. Caird, then mentor of Marcus Borg and N. T. Wright (among others). At Durham I was told I could be mentored by C. K. Barrett, who at the time was probably the best NT scholar in the English-speaking world, and certainly also the most famous Methodist one. The choice of Durham was made easier when I realized that C. E. B. Cranfield was also at Durham and I could sit in on his lectures as well.

Yes, Oxford had a more prestigious reputation among Americans, but in fact all faculties wax and wane over the years, and at that precise time Durham not only had Barrett and Cranfield, they also had the leading expert in Calvin, T. H. L. Parker, John Rogerson in OT and Qumran literature, and many other fine scholars. To my way of thinking, the ensemble of scholars at Durham was stronger than the ones at Oxford.

Now an American student should also realize that the biggest advantage of doing a degree in America is networking. Because of the network of North American scholars, it is easier to get an American job coming out of a doctoral program in America because the letters of recommendation are written by people American institutions will be familiar with—indeed, those with whom scholars at the hiring schools may have personal relationships. Job placement and job interviewing is more difficult if one is abroad. In fact, it often happens that a recommendation from your doctoral supervisor is the key to job placement because the institution in question trusts your supervisor's judgment, and trust is key in hiring an unproven, wet-behind-the-ears person with a PhD.

This fact is somewhat balanced by the enormous good of having a cross-cultural experience. Ann and I loved our years in England and wouldn't trade them for anything. Of course, we quickly learned that America and England are two countries chiefly divided by a common language. Let me explain briefly, using two illustrations from the first year we lived there. The first story really takes the cake!

One day I was in the local bakery in Durham and wanted to order some cake. I got to the front of the line and politely asked the lady, "Can I please have a piece of that cake?"

She replied, "Now lovey, that is the gateau but over here is the cake."

I in turn retorted, "Ma'am, you do realize that 'gateau' is the French word for cake, don't you?"

"Don't be confusing me, son," she replied. "Are you having the gateau or are you having the cake?"

I said, "I'll have the cake which you are calling the gateau."

"Harrumph," she said, and she bagged up a piece of gateau for me.

Then there was the first dinner Ann and I went to at the Methodist manse. The Wallers were the hosts and our clergy couple, and we were both conscious that we needed to be on our best behavior. At one juncture early in the dinner, my wife noticed she did not have anything to wipe her mouth with and asked Carol Waller, "Could I please have a napkin?"

This caused some immediate embarrassment to the hostess and then some whispered conversation in which my poor wife was informed that the word "napkin" in England only referred to either a female sanitary napkin or a baby diaper, called a "nappy." The word used for table napkin in England is the French word "serviette," to prevent confusion. Of course, once Ann was told this, she was so embarrassed that she wanted to crawl under the table.

One of the advantages of doing a dissertation in England is that British English, in contrast to American English, tends to be more formal and less idiomatic, especially if we are talking about the sort of English one would use in writing a scholarly document. One uses the word "one" a lot, for example. This is an advantage because one learns to write in a more formal style, which better suits writing for academic publications.

But something else happens to your own style as well if you live in England for some years. One of my editors has accused me of writing "trans-Atlantic English": one part southern American, one part British. He's right in fact. Your English style is influenced by both what you read and where you read it. I imbibed a lot of English English through conversations and ordinary life in Durham. And sometimes the language barrier was hard to breach.

I remember a conversation early on, after we had moved to Durham, where we had to register with the Constable, the local police. We sat down in the police station, which was only a block from where we lived in the caretaker's house at Elvet Methodist

Church. The man in charge immediately asked, "Do you have any endorsements?"

We looked at each other quizzically, and I said "Endorsements? I didn't know we needed letters of reference to live here."

"No, no," the policemen replied, "I mean endorsements on your driving license."

I was still in a quandary when it finally dawned on me that he was talking about speeding tickets and thus points on my license. I assured him I did not, but it took a while before we communicated clearly with each other in English. It was a good cross-cultural experience to learn a different form of English. In my case, it is one of the things, because it affected my style of writing, that has made my books more accessible to English speakers all over the world. As it turns out, American English is not the gold standard of English in the world, though it is getting there because it is the official language of the Internet these days.

The Mentor

Let's talk about one's doctoral supervisor for a moment. It is important to build a good relationship with your supervisor, but it is also important that you respect the personal-professional boundary. Your doctoral supervisor may be friendly with you, but you must always bear in mind that he is your supervisor and you need to behave accordingly, treating him or her with respect and not in an overly familiar manner. You need the objective judgment of your supervisor in doing your dissertation, and if the relationship becomes too personal, it becomes difficult for the supervisor to give you an honest evaluation.

Kingsley Barrett was an excellent advisor for me, but I quickly learned that in the British system, the professor, in order to encourage you to develop your own critical thinking and your own views, will be reticent, if not abstaining, from telling you what they think about this or that subject or topic. This is rather different from the American system where there is sometimes the tendency for professors to create disciples or clones of themselves who are used as tools to further their own research and interests.

Kingsley Barrett would never do that; indeed, he went out of his way to avoid trying to make me over in his mold or image. Sometimes I got a little frustrated when he would withhold his own opinion on a subject in personal conversation, but in the long run, I realized this was a valuable approach. He didn't want me to run around repeating his thoughts and ideas after him. He wanted me to develop my own voice. One of my fellow students never learned to do this. He was a student of Charles Cranfield, and when he produced a dissertation that basically agreed with Cranfield on almost every point and genuflected in Cranfield's direction, his thesis did not pass.

Eyeing the Competition and the Prize

In any doctoral program, unless it has just started up, you will find yourself thrust into an environment where you will be measured in comparison to your fellow degree-seekers, particularly the ones in the same class and stage of the program as you. Though there will hopefully be some friendly camaraderie, make no mistake that there is competition, sometimes fierce, and you may find yourself saying more than once, "These are the times that try men's and women's souls." You are in a crucible and being tested to see if you are gold or base metal. And sadly, many students do fail the doctoral process.

My advice is not to get too wrapped up in a thousand distractions and make the main thing, the main thing. By this I mean, you did not go to a school to attend endless parties or social functions. Nor did you go there to spend an inordinate amount of time making friends, expanding the size of your family (not generally a good idea when you are living on a subsistence amount of money, such as a grant), or exploring the city, region, or country where you are doing your doctoral work. Yes, you should take breaks, and yes, you need some down time. All work and no play makes Jack a jerk. But at the same time, *beware of displacement activities instead of concentrating hard on researching and writing the dissertation. Beware of working on a PhD in procrastination.*

I watched the thirteen students of C. K. Barrett dwindle down to only three or four actually running the full gauntlet and gaining the prize. The saddest case was the other student I most befriended, who was simply unable to develop his own voice, and so he just repeated the views of his mentor, added nothing new to the discussion of his thesis subject, and failed his Viva. It was heartbreaking. Today, he is a fine minister in Canada, but he could have been a terrific teacher, because I heard him do it. It is never a good thing when a person becomes a preacher by default. What was it the famous man said? "The saddest words of tongue or pen, what might have been, what might have been."

In some ways I would encourage every PhD student to read Rudyard Kipling's poem "If" and take it to heart. You have to persevere and get the degree, no matter what is happening to your fellow students and chums, for the call of God is on your life, and only you can respond to that particular call. No one else can or should do it for you, not even your spouse. Yes, sometimes the ups and downs of PhD work are harder on the spouse than the actual student. They have to suffer in silence, and there is no opportunity for them to shine or be validated or vindicated by this or that famous professor, or by an excellent paper.

PhD programs can be a huge stress on a young marriage, and I have seen a few dissolve, in tears, as a result of the pressure. Before you set your hand to the plow, you had better ask yourself, not just, "Can I do this?" but if you are married, "Can we do this and will it be fair to my spouse to put him or her through this ordeal?" In other words, you need first to assess and count the cost of becoming a "doctor" of the Bible.

Clearing Your Throat: Developing Your Voice

Sometimes people hear the word "critical" and think, "destructive criticism." This, in turn, leads believing folk to have an allergic reaction to the notion of studying the Bible in an academic or scholarly manner. By critical thinking I am talking about the ability to weigh and sift evidence, pro and con, on various subjects that the Bible presents us with. Whether we are talking about the history or interpretation of some text, or the genre of the Gospels, or the nature of prophecy in Revelation, critical thinking is that which weighs the various possibilities and scholarly points of view and draws conclusions based on the evidence and the arguments, rather than on the basis of preconceived notions and commitments.

I am not suggesting that you need to check your Christian faith at the door in order to do critical thinking. My own motto, as noted in the preface, has been that of Anselm: *Fides quaerens intellectum* ("faith seeking understanding"). We must deal honestly with the biblical text and be honest about what we can and cannot know about it on the basis of careful scrutiny and study. We have to be honest enough to say that we don't know this or that, if the evidence is inconclusive or too complex. Suspending judgment is sometimes required.

Just because one is a committed Christian does not mean one has to think it is necessary to have all the answers and to be dogmatic about everything. In fact, if a Christian wants to be a good apologist for the Bible, you must have reasons for the hope that is within you and be able to articulate arguments on behalf of your views. The ability to think critically and then critically engage with other points of view without polemics or ad hominem arguments is part of being a good Christian scholar or teacher.

How about the need to develop one's own voice? By this I do not mean "just be yourself." In a culture of radical individualism, we don't need any encouragement to just be ourselves. Unfortunately some budding scholars have assumed that the essence of being a scholar is simply touting or trumpeting one's own strongly held views, even if they are remarkably eccentric and at odds with the consensus of scholarship. Developing your own voice is not a license to be an oddball or a curmudgeon for Jesus.

What I am talking about is learning to think for yourself, but in a way that is both respectful of other opinions and is prepared to learn from anyone, even from persons with whom you strongly disagree. Even a blind squirrel finds a healthy acorn once in a while, and almost any scholar from any ideological point on the spectrum will have some valuable things to say about the Bible. Furthermore, it is important that you do not allow your piety to outrun the evidence or overrule the pursuit of truth in the service of the truth. Christian Bible scholars above all must be truth seekers. The one who called himself "the truth" is not honored by mere polemics, emotional rhetoric full of sound and fury but without substance, ad hominem arguments, and obscurantism.

Finding one's own voice entails teasing your mind into active thought, learning how to scrutinize the evidence closely, and then evaluating that evidence on your own. You are not developing your own voice if you are just parroting views of your mentors or scholarly heroes. Developing your own voice involves learning how to express what you've learned in an honest, open, and humble way, realizing everyone's knowledge is partial. It involves saying things in your own way and style, but always, always paying attention to other people's views and scholarship and learning from them. And speaking of voice, let's talk about the *viva voce*—the "living voice."

The Living Voice

I turn now to the conclusion of the doctoral dissertating process. Your thesis has been submitted. It's being read by the examiners. In most cases there will be something of an oral defense of your work. Indeed, in the British system the VIVA (from *viva voce*—the "living voice") can be the make-or-break event, not just a pro forma meeting. In my case the VIVA was OK, but it did not go as well as I would have hoped. My external examiner decided it would be better if I rewrote various parts of my thesis so that I would not be preaching to the choir, that is, speaking mainly to those who were already conservative Christians. Both the internal and external examiners had said my research was fine, my conclusions were fine, and so on. They were not objecting to my viewpoint, but they wanted me to argue my case as if I were trying to convince someone who did not already hold my views on the Bible.

At the time I was upset about this, but since then I realized this request for a revision before the final imprimatur could be placed on the dissertation was perhaps the best thing that could have happened to me. It made me realize I needed to write in ways that addressed a much broader audience than just like-minded Christians. I needed to be able to argue for my point of view using evidence and good logic and critical thinking.

I remember immediately after the VIVA going to Kingsley Barrett and asking him why he had not warned me or pushed me to write the dissertation more along the lines that the external examiner was now asking for. He told me he was reluctant or afraid to push me on some critical questions, as he did not want to harm my Christian faith. I later learned that he had had a previous student who came to Durham as an evangelical Anglican and left with no real Christian faith at all. I guess Barrett was worried that history might repeat itself with another of his doctoral students.

Incidentally, the American system of examining dissertations may not involve any external examiners at all; they may all be members of the faculty of the school in which you are matriculating. Then too, in some, but not all American schools there may be feedback from the examiners prior to the oral defense, so there will be no surprises at the oral defense. This is definitely not the case in the British system. The long and short of it is that in the American system there is less to worry about when it comes to the oral defense, but in the British system the external examiner at the oral defense has so much weight, that he can derail your obtaining the degree if you do not have a good oral defense.

In any case, so it was that for the next year of my life, I revised my dissertation accordingly, arguing my case, not merely assuming it. Ann and I moved to rural North Carolina (an experience she called "culture-less shock" after living in Durham in the shadow of a Norman cathedral), and we pastored four Methodist churches and raised our infant daughter, Christy, who had been born in Durham, England. This was a lot to have on my plate at once, but God was good.

The dissertation got revised, it passed muster, it was immediately accepted into the Cambridge Monograph Series, and in fact it became the bestselling Cambridge monograph in that Society of

New Testament Studies series up to that point in time. *Women in the Ministry of Jesus* did so well that they wanted the rest of the dissertation in another monograph, *Women in the Earliest Churches*. With the success of those two monographs, all sorts of publishers were prepared to entertain possible writing projects of mine.

Besides revising those two monographs for a more popular audience in *Women and the Genesis of Christianity*, I moved on to a real heart project—writing about Jesus. The first such effort was a book with Fortress Press entitled *The Christology of Jesus*, dealing with Jesus' self-understanding, a book that is still in print and selling twenty years later. This led to five more books about Jesus! But then John 21:25 did warn us that the world could not contain the full number of Jesus books if everything he ever said and did was written down.

Publishing the Dissertation, and Publishers

These last two paragraphs have been written to show you what can happen if you write and revise a good dissertation for publication. Bear in mind that a good dissertation is only your first effort at scholarly work, and most everyone will evaluate it that way. You don't have to spring from the head of Zeus fully formed, to use a classics metaphor, when it comes to your dissertation. You simply have begun the process of being a good Bible scholar.

You should not let a good beginning, including the publishing of the dissertation, get in the way of getting on with developing as a scholar, doing more and different research so that you don't become famous as "Johnny One Note," a person who had nothing to say or contribute to the scholarly discussion beyond the dissertation. A good beginning is not an ending or an end in itself. It's just a good beginning, and you need to continue to do original research as a scholar if you are going to grow as a teacher and scholar, and especially if you are called to be not just a teacher but also a publishing scholar.

Let's talk for a moment about publishers. There are a lot of them, and whom you seek out as a publisher will depend in part on how you view the ministry you are called to do. For example, suppose you are a conservative Christian scholar, but you feel called to work in a secular university. If that's your calling, you had better not be mainly or firstly publishing with presses known as conservative Christian publishers. You need, for example, to get your dissertation published by a university press or the equivalent.

But suppose your calling is to teach at a genuinely Christian college or seminary, not merely a "church-related" school that has long since left behind a dominantly Christian ethos. Then, it may be fine to publish with one or more of the evangelical publishing houses. It all depends on the ministry you are called to by God. In my case, I am ordained in a mainline denomination, and I felt from the outset that it was my task to try and speak to as large an audience as possible, not just to fellow conservative Christians. This is why I have published with university presses, evangelical presses, large secular presses that also do religious publishing (e.g., Harper), and so on. You need to have a clear sense of what God is asking of you in terms of your scholarship before you decide what avenue to pursue in terms of a publisher.

I will say again that in my case, it was providential that my external examiner at Durham demanded revisions and more critical thinking on my part. I would not have been able to do the Wesleyan job of trying to serve the world as my parish, and all sorts of audiences as my listeners, had that not happened to me. I would be more likely to have only been able to say "my parish is my world." It was serendipity that happened in my life in 1980, and God worked it together for good, using it to open up doors that would otherwise have been closed to me.

In the next few chapters, I want to talk more specifically about how you equip yourself to be a biblical scholar, apart from just picking a school or a mentor or a dissertation topic. I will talk about the tools that need to be in a teacher's or scholar's toolbox if they are going to be good at being a Bible teacher or scholar. The next chapter will be about the genesis of such preparation, as we go back *ad fontes*. But first I want to share a little meditation on inertia—on the sort of self-talk that can prevent you from becoming all God wants you to be.

IF ONLY

I

I would have dressed up,
Only it was too much trouble.
I would have gone out,
Only it cost too much.
I would have driven,
Only travel's dangerous.
I would have eaten,
Only I weigh too much.
I would have danced,
Only I didn't have a partner.
I would have returned,
Only it brought back bad memories.

II

I would have gone,
Only I didn't have time.
I would have visited,
Only I wasn't wanted.
I would have tried,
Only it was a waste of energy.
I would have helped,
Only they didn't need me.
I would have cared,
Only I didn't feel like it.
I would have cried,
Only I wasn't sorry.

III

I would have volunteered,
Only I had better things to do.
I would have voted,
Only it wouldn't have changed things.
I would have donated,
Only they'd made their quota.
I would have spoken up,

Only I was afraid to.
I would have acted,
Only others got there first.
I would have felt sorry,
Only I didn't feel guilty.

IV

I would have prepared,
Only it was too much work.
I would have studied,
Only I wouldn't have passed.
I would have corrected it,
Only it was too late.
I would have told the truth,
Only it would have offended.
I would have graduated,
Only life intervened.
I would have gotten the job,
Only they didn't like me.

V

I would have prayed,
Only God only knows.
I would have worshipped,
Only I hate to sing.
I would have fellowshipped
Only I didn't know them.
I would have served,
Only I didn't have the calling.
I would have loved,
Only it hurt too much.
I would have lived,
If only.

BW III
January 20, 2006

3

AD FONTES:
BACK TO THE SOURCE(S)

An Intimate, Intimidating Seminar

It was a chilly day in Durham, England, and I was making my regular climb up the hill, along the cobblestone streets, past the medieval cathedral to Abbey House on Palace Green, in order to attend C. K. Barrett's famous New Testament seminar. This seminar was not a listed course but rather a high-powered, by-invitation-only gathering of faculty and doctoral students to study some particular book of the New Testament or another piece of early Christian literature. The little conference room had a long rectangular table in the middle of it surrounded by chairs, which, in turn, were surrounded by bookshelves full of musty books. Already piled on the table were various lexicons and reference tools. As the scholars and doctoral students shuffled in, each took a predetermined seat.

It was my duty to sit to the right of the former Archbishop of Canterbury, Lord Michael Ramsay, who held his ancient Greek text in his trembling hands carefully as if he were holding a baby. To his left was C. E. B. Cranfield, who was finishing the ICC Romans commentary at that juncture; to his left was George Dragas, a patristics scholar in the department whose expertise was in the *Apostolic Constitutions*. At the head of the table was Kingsley Barrett himself, presiding as it were, over this conclave. On the other side of the table was Professor Ann Loades, on this day visiting NT scholar W. D. Davies, several other students, and T. H. L. Parker, the great Reformation expert and translator of Calvin's commentaries. To say this was a daunting company would be putting it mildly. And today was my day to translate from the *Didache* and offer a possible interpretation of the Greek passage in question.

Barrett cleared his throat and said, "As is our way, we must begin *ad fontes*, going back to the original sources in the original languages, and in this case this fall we continue to study that intriguing little early Christian document called *The Teaching of the Twelve Apostles*, or *The Didache*. It is Mr. Witherington's turn to translate for us the passage about the Lord's Supper."

With that, I took a deep breath, and launched into a rather literal translation of the aforementioned passage, reading from my Loeb classical library edition of the Apostolic Fathers. Though there was an English translation on the facing page, I was not allowed to use it but had to do my own. "*Ad fontes,*" Barrett had said—back to the source, the original language text. In his mind there was no possible substitute for that exercise, whether one was reading the New Testament or some other early Christian book. I had heard this before when I did summer study with Bruce Metzger at Princeton in the Apostolic Fathers.

When I had finished the translation, Barrett, peering around the huge bushy eyebrows of Lord Ramsay, stared at me and said, "And what do you make of that passage?" I offered a tentative explanation; but Barrett wasn't satisfied, so he pressed me, "And what *precisely* do you mean by that?" He asked with some vigor, but without any malice. There was one part of this rather young Carolina boy that wanted to say, "Honest sir, I didn't mean nothing by that," but I sallied forth and gave a faltering answer. What I really wanted to do about then was crawl under the table and hide. It was an intimidating setting in which to learn Greek better.

Foreign Languages—Culture's Gateway

We all know the saying, "It's all Greek to me," by which is meant, it's in a foreign language I don't know. Language is the gateway into any culture, whether ancient or modern. It does not tell you everything you might want to know about the culture, but it is the starting point for those wanting to understand a culture well. I was fortunate and blessed to have had an education in High Point, North Carolina, in the 1950s and 1960s in which original language study was deemed just as important as math and science. I'm afraid those days are long gone in most American schools, and it is a great loss for those who want to be serious students of the Bible.

In the third grade we began learning Spanish, and in junior high I took Latin and loved it. I continued it into my high school years, and one of my best teachers in high school was my Latin teacher, Ms. Phillips. I owe her a lot. She inspired in me a love of ancient languages, which still burns bright in my soul. So much was this the case that when I went off to Carolina, while I took the required modern language (French), what I was really keen to do was take ancient Greek, so I could read both the Latin and Greek classics.

My study of Greek at UNC began with Xenophon and ended with the NT. Meanwhile I also took Greek history (in this case, Alexander the Great), and it was indeed great—Jim McCoy, the Greek history teacher, made it all come alive. I was fired up! It was just about that time that Dr. Bernard Boyd got hold of me and got me to focus on the Bible, particularly the Greek New Testament. My course had now begun to be charted toward becoming a Bible scholar. It all begins with languages—in fact, several ancient and modern languages.

I cannot emphasize enough how important and how exciting it is to read the Bible in its original languages and to watch the text come alive right before your eyes. There is no substitute for original language study of any ancient text. A translation of the Bible is no different than a translation of Homer's *Odyssey*, no matter how good the translation actually is. A translation is already an interpretation of the text, for words and phrases in any language have multiple possible meanings, and judgment calls have to be made about the meaning of this or that word, this or that phrase. And there are idioms that cannot be translated literally from one language to another.

As the old saying goes, something gets lost in translation. Indeed it does. Some of the original meaning often gets lost, and in place of it, we too quickly and anachronistically insert our modern meanings into the text. If languages are not your gift, or at least not something you are prepared to work hard on, then abandon any hope at becoming a good biblical scholar, or a good graduate or post-graduate level teacher of the Bible. You cannot get around the language requirement. If you can't go "back to the font," you will never drink from the original spring water and find the refreshment and enlightenment it provides.

One of the things that worries me most about education in biblical studies these days, both at the college and at the seminary levels, is that in my lifetime schools have so dumbed down the curriculum that original language study in the biblical languages is no longer, or not much, required. This is even true at some of our elite colleges and seminaries-in-America. It's an astounding and discouraging fact. There was a day when one could not become a minister or teacher in some denominations without a working knowledge of the biblical languages.

But the goal of training someone to be a scholar pastor or teaching pastor has largely fallen by the wayside in the rush to be more "relevant" to modern concerns, anxieties, and cultural trends. We are paying a steep price for it—shoddy Bible teaching, superficial sermons that hardly engage the meat of the Word, bad pastoral counseling based on a misunderstanding of biblical texts, and the like. It's a sad state of affairs, but it does not have to be that way.

Jeff, one of my students when I was teaching at Ashland Theological Seminary, really struggled with languages, but he understood their importance. Ashland had not compromised its integrity when it came to languages. The students still had to take some Greek and Hebrew in order to get their MDiv degree. Jeff had failed Hebrew twice, and he was pursuing ordination in the United Methodist Church. His district superintendent had suggested he transfer to a Methodist school near Columbus and finish his degree there, "where you don't have to run the gauntlet of all those biblical languages and you can still get your MDiv degree."

Jeff refused. He had concluded he needed to fight the good fight and pass the language course if he was going to be a good pastor who "rightly divides the Word of truth." He wanted to be able to read good commentaries on the Bible and recognize the words and phrases in the original languages that the commentator was discussing. Thus, he took Hebrew for a third time, and this time he passed—by the hair of his chinny chin chin. On the day of the graduation ceremony, when Jeff walked across the stage to get his MDiv diploma, many of us stood and applauded Jeff, with tears in our eyes. He had taken the road less travelled by, and it has made a big difference in his ministry going forward. He is a good expositor of God's Word, using his knowledge of its original languages and meanings.

Idioms, Not Idiots

It's not just a matter of learning vocabulary either. Idioms especially get lost in translation. For instance, let's take the phrase from Acts 26:14: "It hurts you to kick against the goads" (NRSV). A goad is a stick with some sharp point or pointy object on it, used as something of a cattle prod. We still have the English phrase, "You goaded me into it," though most modern English-speaking persons probably do not know what a "goad" was. But in fact, the idiom here is not talking about literal cattle prods; rather, it refers to how futile it is to resist God and God's plan for your life. Indeed, it hurts when you run into the brick wall called God when God opposes something you are doing.

This idiom, which in the NRSV is translated literally as "it hurts you to kick against the goads," requires explanation in English because we don't use that idiom in English. The meaning is lost in translation if the translation is literal. This provides a parade example of why simply using a literal translation of the Bible without good commentaries to help interpret the Greek text is insufficient for teaching or preaching God's Word.

Idioms are funny things. If I call up my friend Klaus in Tübingen, Germany, and say literally in Deutsch, "Klaus, I have an axe to grind," he is going to think I have become a lumberjack. German, unlike English, doesn't use that idiom to mean, "He has an agenda."

Each language has its own idiomatic phrases and peculiar words. It just shows how important original language study is to becoming a real Bible scholar.

The Quandry of Cain

Ralph Cain was mentally challenged. But he was also a committed Christian in his forties with a very sweet spirit when I knew him. He lived with his elderly momma Claddy near Coleridge, North Carolina. One day, as pastor of four rural United Methodist churches, I went to visit the Cains. I remember vividly sitting in their front room and Ralph had his old dog-eared King James Bible in his hand. He had been memorizing some of the psalms, and something had stumped him.

Turning to Psalm 23, his favorite Psalm (mine too), he said, "Dr. Ben, it says here 'The Lord is my shepherd, I shall not want,' and I don't get that. I mean, I want him, so why does it say, 'I shall not want'?"

It was a perfectly honest question, and so I simply explained, "Ralph, the problem here is the old English you are reading this in. What the text means is, 'If God is your shepherd, you will lack for nothing essential.'"

Ralph's face lit up like a Christmas tree as the real meaning of the text dawned on him, and he replied, "I just knew it couldn't mean I didn't want him, 'cause I do."

There are a lot of obstacles to understanding the text of the Bible—some of them modern, some of them ancient. In the case of Ralph Cain, the problem was using an outdated ancient translation that used the word "want" in a way that we in the twenty-first century don't use any more. English is a living language, and the problem with using old translations from the early seventeenth century is that the language has moved on, and words and phrases have changed meanings over time. The Bible is hard enough to interpret for the ordinary reader without the additional complication of reading it in antique English. You need a good recent translation to begin to penetrate the text's meaning, if you can't read the Bible in its original languages.

Keeping Languages Alive: The Juggling Game

You may be saying, however: "Who is sufficient for these things? How do you keep a knowledge of an ancient language fresh in your mind?" The truth is, you can't keep any language, modern or ancient, fresh in your mind unless you regularly use those languages. Keeping languages alive in your head is a bit like juggling multiple balls—in my case, it means juggling Hebrew, Aramaic, Greek, French, Latin, and German, in addition to my native English. Unless you have a photographic memory and/or a real gift for languages, the truth is your languages are constantly in a state of flux—of going in and out of usability and freshness. Right now my Hebrew is a bit rusty because I have not had to use it on a daily basis since I stopped teaching the OT when I came to Asbury. Yes, with a lexicon I can do alright, but my sight reading isn't what it once was. In short, keeping languages going is a matter of continuing to use them on a regular basis, whatever language we are talking about.[3]

Sometimes young people who want to become Bible teachers and Bible scholars assume that what is meant is that they must learn how to speak these languages fluently. This assumption is, of course, based on the way we learn languages like Spanish, French, or German in American schools. Conversational French or conversational Spanish has to be an essential part of the training. For a biblical scholar this is useful but not necessary. What is needed is a particular kind of knowledge of such languages whether ancient or modern—a reading knowledge of the language.

To be more specific, a Bible scholar needs to know a specific subset of German or French called theological German or theological French. In other words, there is a lot of specialty vocabulary and phrases one needs to know to read an exegetical or theological article in the aforementioned languages. And if you are reading an ancient language like Koine Greek, you need to know how early Christians used the language theologically and ethically. There will be special nuances and vocabulary in that case. Let's take an example.

The Greek word group *sōtēria/sōtēr/sōzō* can be translated salvation/savior/to save, but what that word group refers to in most

---

3. For help with Greek, for example, see Constantine R. Campbell's book *Keep Your Greek: Strategies for Busy People* (Grand Rapids: Zondervan, 2010).

ancient Greek literature is not to give someone the gift of everlasting life, or the result of having that gift, or the person who gave you that gift. Rather, it usually means is to "help," to "heal," to "rescue" from danger. And to make this matter more complicated, even in the NT there are times when the less theological meaning of this language is used. For example when Jesus heals the woman with the long-term flow of blood in her body, he says, "Daughter, your faith has saved you"; but what he likely means is, "Your faith has healed you." Jesus is not referring to his having given her the gift of eternal life because she now believes in Jesus. The text likely has a less theologically loaded meaning.

Studying the original languages, then, in order to become a good teacher or scholar of the Bible is a commitment to lifelong dealing with these languages, learning of these languages, and refreshing and relearning of these languages. But the good news is that you don't have to learn to *speak* all these languages, nor do you need to know all the vocabulary possible in these languages, just the subset that is required for your understanding the Bible and the scholarly work on the Bible.

The ancients believed that the eyes of a person are the windows on their souls. If you had good keen eyes, you must have a good, clear, keen soul. Languages are kind of like that—they are the windows into a culture, including an ancient culture. Like windows they don't tell you everything about what's inside the culture. They are just means through which you can more clearly view those cultures. For those who don't learn the necessary languages, these windows are opaque; a person can look at the words but see nothing. Indeed, they might be in danger of seeing their own reflection rather than looking into the world of another culture.

The call of Kingsley Barrett, "Let's go *ad fontes*"—that is, to the original sources—is still ringing in my ears. No matter how many commentaries you read, theologies you study, histories you ponder, if you do not study the requisite languages, you have settled for taking other people's words for the meaning of this or that sentence, phrase, or word. You have settled for the use of secondary sources. Secondary sources are necessary, but they are no substitute for God's Word in its original languages; they should only be supplements to original language study, because the Bible's instruction to "study to find yourself approved" is referring to your own direct engagement with the original language biblical text. It is about that original language text that 2 Timothy 3:16 reminds us, "All Scripture is God-breathed." Any translation of the Bible is just that—one step removed from the original, and already an interpretation.

Moses on Mount Sinai, you may remember, was bold enough to ask to see God's face. God did not allow that, as it would have destroyed Moses; but God did give him his Word in Hebrew to give to the people. It is the privilege and the duty of a true Bible teacher or a scholar to give the Word of God to their charges—not just a translation, but the Word itself. But this requires that such a person has himself first gone to drink from the fountain, from the intoxicating life-giving water. There's nothing like it, and there is no substitute if you want to be a teacher or a scholar of God's Word. Language is the window into the ancient culture. It can also be the key that opens the door to the house.

The Language Barrier

I was at the airport in Cairo with my tour group, and we were trying to get into Egypt. I was at the head of our group's line, and there was a problem with my passport. It was an older, but not out-of-date passport, and the passport picture showed me sporting a moustache, whereas in 1995 when this trip took place, I no longer had one. The passport control agent looked at me, and then down at the passport, and then back at me, and then down at the passport, and said, "Is you? No, is not you."

When he reiterated this for the second time, I finally smiled and said, "Salaam Aleichum" ("peace to you" in Arabic). His face lit up and he said, "You know Arabic: it must be you!" and he firmly stamped the passport and let me in with a smile. Language can be the window, even the key into a foreign world and foreign culture. But knowing languages is only the starting point for being a Bible teacher or scholar. In the next chapter we need to discuss ancient cultures and contexts themselves.

WORDSHAPED

Partial and piecemeal, here and there
Vowels omitted, consonants square
No jots or tittles, not one iota
As if there was some sort of letter quota.

Line upon line, word for word
Nopunctuationseparationabsurd
Scriptum continuum without an end
Space is so precious, conventions must bend.

Fair hand copy, stylus in hand
Awaiting dictation, write on demand
Line length is even, no letters odd
So it must be — the Word of God.

Written revelation, unveiled truth
Put on papyrus, sold from a booth
Unroll the scroll, unseal the seal
Meant to inform, not to conceal.

Nomina sacra, the Holy Name
In abbreviation, meaning the same
IX, XC, IHS too
Jehovah combines, God's name times two.

Inspired authors, inspiring text
God breathed words, soul resurrects
Let it be written, let it be done
Fulfilling fulfillment, victory won.

In the beginning, God chose to speak
Creation created, in under a week
Even the last Word, God will have too
Alpha-Omega, indwelling you.

BW III
March 26, 2006

4

PRIMING THE PUMP:
ORIGINAL CONTEXT STUDY

Context Is King

Let's suppose now that you can read the Bible in its original languages. What is the second step to understanding the Bible? The answer is, understanding the Bible in its original contexts and cultures. If language is a window on an ancient culture, you must do more than just look through the window. You need to go into the front door of the ancient house and walk around and take stock of its character. This involves first a knowledge of ancient religious, social, and cultural history, and some knowledge of what archaeology and epigraphy and other sciences have revealed about the biblical cultures. As I have already said, "A text without a context is just a pretext for whatever you want it to mean." We need to understand the Bible in its original contexts, because as one person once said, "The past is like a foreign country; they do things differently there."

Let's talk, then, about the ways biblical culture is different from modern Western culture. There are many differences besides just language differences. One obvious major difference is that the ancients didn't live in democratic societies or capitalistic economies. It's a mistake to assume they did and thereby assume that the Bible is the basis of such modern forms of viewing the world and modern ways for people to relate to one another. The democracies of ancient Greece were long gone by the time we get to the NT era, and even during the OT era, they did not affect the lands the Hebrews were involved in. They lived in tribal and monarchial cultures.

As for ancient economies, they were basically barter economies, with money only beginning to be a major means of exchange by the time we get to the NT era. In any case the backbone of these ancient economies was not blue collar or white collar workers, or the middle class. Indeed, the phrase "middle class" really describes no one in antiquity. There were the über-rich (about 4 to 5 percent of the population), and then there was everyone else. Including slaves. Lots of slaves.

The Roman empire to a large extent ran on slave labor—quite literally. One estimate says that almost 40 percent of the population of Rome in Paul's day were slaves![4] It is no surprise, then, that we have lengthy passages in Colossians 3 and Ephesians 6, plus the whole letter of Philemon, that deal with the problems caused by slavery. Paul is all in favor of slaves being manumitted, as Philemon makes clear. Indeed, he sees incompatibility between being someone's slave and being that same person's brother in Christ.

This brings us to an important reminder: even when you learn and understand the nature of ancient cultures and how they differ from modern ones, you still have to assess whether and in what ways early Christianity was moving *against the grain* of the culture, moving in a countercultural way. But you must first know what the dominant cultural assumptions were to begin with, before you can assess a possible countercultural response.

Against the Grain

Besides the reaction to slavery, another good example of New Testament writers moving against the grain of the ancient culture is the way they respond to the patriarchy of all these biblical cultures. There is no doubt that these ancient societies were male-dominated societies. This did not mean women might not in some cases play important religious, political, social, or business roles. They often did. But that was not the dominant character of day-to-day life in ancient society. It was a world where men had almost all the advantages, especially when it came to public and nonfamilial roles.

---

4. See my commentary *Conflict and Community in Corinth* (Grand Rapids: Eerdmans, 1995).

It is all the more striking, then, that in the NT we find Jesus and Paul and others going out of their ways to affirm new religious and social roles for women; furthermore, they work on reforming the existing patriarchal family structure. How so? (1) Men could no longer divorce their wives and see that as a male privilege. (2) Women were no longer required to be in a marital relationship; it was appropriate to remain single for the sake of the kingdom. (3) The roles of the head of the household were severely attenuated in the Christian household codes so that the husband-father-master had all sorts of new Christian strictures placed on how he should relate to other members of the family. Indeed, Paul is even bold enough to say that the goal was mutual submission of all Christians to one another in the body of Christ (Eph. 5:20–21).

In other words, simply recognizing the strongly patriarchal character of ancient culture is not enough. The question is how Christians like Paul seek to qualify, change, or modify those dominant cultural structures by putting the leaven of the gospel into the extant lump of society as it was expressed in the Christian household and the Christian church meetings.

Against Our Prevailing Wind

Some of the major cultural building blocks of ancient society do indeed go against most modern assumptions about life. For example, modern Western culture assumes that individualism is a good thing. You can even see signs at Christian college campuses that say, "Accent on the individual." The problem with this approach is it is largely unbiblical, and in some cases one could call it antibiblical.

Notice how the characters in the gospels do not have last names. The cell phone logs must have been really confusing—Saul is Saul of Tarsus, Jesus is Jesus of Nazareth, and I am trusting you know that Mary's last name was not Magdalene. In fact, she was Miryam of Migdal. People with the same personal names would be distinguished not by a demarcating last name, like we use to individuate things, but rather by a point of geographical origin, by a size (John the little), by a patronymic (Simon bar Jonah), or by a religious affiliation (Simon the Pharisee, Simon the Zealot).

People's identities were bound up not in what distinguished them from the crowd but rather what crowd they were a part of.

Anthropologists call this dyadic personality, or group-based identity. Ancient peoples were certainly individuals, but they didn't much believe in individualism. Their identities were shaped by geography, generation (who's your Daddy), and gender, and by what groups they were members of (ethnic groups—Jews vs. Gentiles; religious groups—pagans vs. Jews or Christians). Have you noticed that even the titles of Christ are relational terms, telling us who Jesus is in relationship to God the Father (Son of God, the Messiah/Anointed One of God) or human beings (Son of Man), or later in relationship to his followers (Savior, Lord)?

Having said this, it is true that we start seeing some emphasis on being an individual in the conversion language of the NT ("if anyone is in Christ, the new creation has come," 2 Cor. 5:17 NRSV). But in fact, most ancient peoples didn't believe in the concept of conversion. They didn't believe a leopard could change its spots. Nicodemus's response in John 3 to Jesus' mention of second birth was not merely surprise, but incredulity. The only rebirth he thought Jesus must be referring to was crawling back into a mother's womb and calling for womb service again! The earliest followers of Jesus certainly did believe that by the Spirit of God a person could be changed, both in terms of religious orientation and in terms of character and ethics. One's personality might remain the same, but character and behavior were another matter.

The Reciprocity Cycle

Another good example from the study of social history is the way ancient societies were reciprocity cultures: you scratch my back and I'll scratch yours. Perhaps you will remember the famous scene from the *Godfather* movie (Part One), where Marlon Brando, playing Don Corleone, the Godfather himself, tells the man standing before him, "You will do me a favor, after which I will do you a favor, then you will do me another favor ... or you will sleep with the fish." The man in question clearly had no choice but to be stuck in the reciprocity cycle.

In a world of patrons and clients, rather than merely businesspersons and customers, the clients always found themselves "beholden" to their patron and caught in the web of reciprocity, with no easy way out of it. We do have some of this in modern Western society. We even have clichés like "you don't get something for nothing." The ancient world was characterized by pecking orders, stratification, and reciprocity conventions that were used to keep people, particularly clients, in their place, "owing their souls to the company store" (to borrow a phrase from an old Tennessee Ernie Ford song). Into this world came a message of grace, of unmerited favor, of undeserved benefit. Not surprisingly, people were suspicious of it. They still are today, though perhaps less so than in antiquity.

Dr. Richard Halverson was an important person in my college years. At the time he was the pastor of the Fourth Presbyterian Church in Bethesda, Maryland, where my roommate and good friend Rick Sanders attended when he went home from Carolina. Dr. Halverson once told a story of a wealthy person in his congregation whom he took out to dinner one day just to have some fellowship with the man. Now this man was a charitable soul, a real sacrificial giver, but it was also the case that he was used to being "hit up" for money by this or that well-meaning person. So when the dinner was over, the man pushed back his chair from the table and said to Dick Halverson, "So, tell me Dick, what do you want?" The man assumed that Pastor Halverson had taken him out to dinner to proposition him or plead for some money for some worthy church cause. Dick Halverson's response came as something of a shock.

"I don't want anything from you: I just wanted fellowship with you," said Dick. The man broke down and cried. He was so used to being used, to being caught up in the cycle of giving and receiving that when a moment of pure grace happened in his life, he could hardly believe it. It must have been even harder to believe in grace in Jesus' world, a truly payback kind of world, especially in view of all the rivalry and enmity conventions that set off endless cycles of reprisals, or (on the positive side) reciprocal gift giving. Grace must have been seen as a total miracle in various contexts in the ancient world.

There is much more we could say about ancient social history and its differences from and similarities to modern Western social culture, but this must suffice because we need to talk about religious history and even political history, and how different the worlds of the Bible were from our world.

Religion and Politics

One of the usual caricatures of the Pharisees, even to this day in the church, is that they were a bunch of legalistic hypocrites, all straining over gnats and swallowing camels. They are perceived as the ultimate nitpickers. Of course, like most caricatures, there are some ancient Pharisees who doubtless could sit for that portrait and it would resemble them. Jesus wasn't critiquing ghosts when he accused some Pharisees of hypocrisy, of saying one thing and doing another, of placing the emphasis on the wrong syllable in the law, and so on. At the same time, there were clearly plenty of good, pious Pharisees; for example, Nicodemus would seem to fall in that category.

If you don't know the history of Pharisaism from before the time of Jesus and the history of early Judaism after the disaster of the destruction of the temple in AD 70, you will not be able to see what Jesus is really critiquing. You won't understand Paul either; furthermore, you might well make the common modern mistake of reading later rabbinic Judaism back into the situation of Jesus and Paul prior to AD 70.

This is, indeed, a big mistake on both ends of the spectrum. In addition, there is another reason why one needs to know well the religious context in which Jesus and his followers operated. The only major group of Jews that survived and thrived after AD 70 were the Pharisees, and they are the basis of all modern forms of Judaism. Whereas before AD 70 Judaism had focused on torah, temple, and territory, after 70, and especially after the squelching of the Bar Kokhba revolt in the second century AD, Judaism by necessity became increasingly a Torah-centric religion.

What of political history? If you want to understand the zealots, including zealots like Saul of Tarsus, you must understand the Maccabean period before the time of Christ. If you want to understand the death of Jesus on a Roman cross, you have to know some political history of Rome. If you want to understand the importance of Paul having Roman citizenship, you need to know something about ancient Roman citizenship. If you want to understand Herod the Great's temple and his various other building projects, or Herod Antipas's beheading of John the Baptizer, you have to understand ancient politics in the Holy Land.

The tendency to overspiritualize the Bible and ignore its social, religious, or political historical contexts is a mistake, and it leads to errors in judgment when reading the Bible. These sorts of errors of judgment, including the error of anachronism, are avoidable with enough contextual study of the Bible; like the language requirement, the contextual study of the Bible is an absolute must if you wish to become either a Bible teacher or a Bible scholar. One of the reasons I have written so many socio-rhetorical commentaries on the NT is precisely because I realized how vital the social, religious, and rhetorical contexts are to a correct reading and interpretation of the Bible.[5]

Digging the Context

What about archaeology? It is apparently fashionable these days to suggest that archaeology doesn't "prove" the Bible, by which is usually meant that the specific persons and events in the Bible can't be confirmed through archaeology. We seldom dig up something like the James ossuary, the burial box of Jesus' brother, something that has a direct connection with a historical figure mentioned in the Bible.

As true as that is, archaeology is crucial to getting a clearer picture of the economic, social, religious, and political contexts in which Jesus and his followers operated. Such data provides a corrective against all sorts of modern assumptions we might make about the biblical text. It is one of the reasons I have spent so much time in the lands of the Bible crawling over archaeological sites and talking to archaeologists.

---

5. See the various volumes in the series of commentaries I have done for Eerdmans and for InterVarsity Press.

I am not an archaeologist or the son of an archaeologist, nor do I play one on TV—you know what they say about archaeologists, their lives are constantly in ruins. You don't have to be an archaeologist to be a Bible scholar, but you must read the reports and pay attention to the data archaeologists bring to the surface because history matters! Judaism and Christianity are historical religions, grounded in specific cultures, with specific histories at specific points in time. If Christianity were merely some sort of spiritual gumbo for the soul, some sort of philosophy of life, history might not matter. But that is not Christianity. At the heart of Christianity is the life, death, and resurrection of a historical person named Jesus, and the more one knows about his historical context, the better one can know the man in various regards. History matters, and its subset—archaeology—matters as well.

For example, archaeological work has shown us a good deal about the structure of first-century Jewish homes. One of the most frequent designs was that the home had a large front room that served as the dining and family room, a bedroom off to the right of the door that could serve as the guest room, a further bedroom toward the right back of the house, and at the very back of the house a petition wall, behind which would be kept the family's beast of burden or most precious animal.

The guest room was called the *katalyma*, the very word used to describe the room where Jesus would eat the Passover with his disciples in Jerusalem (see Luke 22:11). It is this very same word that we find in the birth narrative story in Luke 2:7. When Luke wants to refer to a roadside inn, he uses a different Greek word: *pandocheion* (Luke 10:34). In short, the crucial verse in the birth narrative, based on both the linguistic and the archaeological evidence, should read, "and they placed the baby in the manger, because there was no room in the guest room." In other words, Jesus was likely born in the back of the ancestral home in Bethlehem. The family had arrived too late to have the guest room, and the only place they could be put was in the back of the house. All these sermons about "no room in the inn" are not based on sound study of the linguistic and archaeological context of the story in Luke 2.

Those scriptural stories and their words do not have meaning in isolation. They have meaning in contexts. And it is not true that "in the beginning was the dictionary." Dictionaries are compilations of words that have been studied in their various contexts to discover the range of their meanings. There is no choice for a Bible teacher or Bible scholar but to study the Bible in light of its various original contexts, if you want to understand the meaning of God's Word. Otherwise, you will continue to commit the error of reading the Bible anachronistically — over and over and over again.

There is, however, another sort of context that the budding teacher or scholar must pay attention to and be trained in, in order to be a good teacher or scholar. That is the literary contexts of the Bible, and we will turn to that subject in our next chapter. First, however, a meditation on the importance of spending time in the original contexts in which the Bible was written — in the case of this poem, in Jerusalem, at the Wailing Wall.

CRACKS IN THE WALL

Cracks in the wall,
There by design,
Prayers on plain paper
One of them mine

Rabbis are chanting,
Torah held high,
Sunlight is fading,
In the blue sky.

Guards are watching,
Passing the time,
Nodding acquaintance
With the sublime.

Herod's temple,
All that remains
Limestone platform,
Withstands the strain,

Mosque's gold dome
Shines in the light,
Whose God is honored
By what's in sight?

Prayers of the righteous
Meant to be heard,
But the papers are silent,
Don't speak a word.

"We want messiah"
Yeshiva boy cries,
The irony is thick,
And darkens the skies

Christians with kepas
Stand by the shrine,
Praying to Jesus,
As someone divine.

The wailing wall,
Heard Jesus' lament
That he would have gathered,
If Zion repents.

Cracks in the wall,
Filled up with our prayers,
Perhaps it is this,
Which keeps God right there.
Perhaps when Messiah
Comes (once again),
Perhaps then the Spirit
Will descend through the air,
Perhaps then true monotheists
Will kneel at God's feet,

Be filled with his Spirit,
The Father's Son greet.

True children of Abram
Meet at the wall
And confess Trinity,
The One for us all.
Is this a dream—we three
could be one?
Just as God is,
Whose plan is not done.
"Something there is
That doesn't like a wall"
But this one unites
The One with us all.

BW III
September 11, 2005

5

ARE YOU LITERATE IN LITERATURE?
THE IMPORTANCE OF LITERARY SENSITIVITY

It is not possible to draw up a one-size-fits-all description of the sort of preparation a person needs to become a Bible teacher or a Bible scholar. Different people go down different roads to arrive at that destination. There are easier and harder ways to get there. One of the problems occurs when someone tries to become a Bible teacher or scholar with serious deficiencies in their education or abilities.

In an age of overspecialization, these deficiencies can be masked or disguised, at least for a while—just long enough to get a job, for example. I have known doctoral students who did their doctoral dissertations on such minutia as "the use of the connective δέ in compound Greek sentences." While this is not an unimportant subject when it comes to understanding Greek grammar, it hardly prepares you for the task of teaching Bible at colleges and seminaries. You will quickly discover that you cannot simply read your dissertation day after day in class. You will have to teach a variety of subjects, and in some of them you may be only a week or two ahead of your students!

In other words, to become an effective Bible teacher, you must become a general practitioner of the field of biblical studies. You will need as broad an education as you can get.

Literary Literacy

Bible scholars need a background in literature and in how to study literature. You need to have a degree of literary sensitivity to read and interpret the Bible because the Bible is a compendium of all kinds of different literature—poetry, prose, narrative, songs, laws, proverbs, parables, prophecies, apocalyptic discourse, and much more. To know the conventions of this or that genre of literature is a key to knowing the possibilities and limitations of interpreting certain passages in the Bible. But how do you develop such sensitivity? As a bare beginning, you need to read good literature, both ancient and modern.

If you read good modern English literature and absorb it, it will help you become a more articulate person and a better writer. We could use some better writers among biblical teachers and scholars. Too much of what passes for lesson plans for classes in Bible, and textbooks for those classes, is dull as dishwater and twice as murky. Not everyone who is a Bible teacher needs to be able to write with literary finesse. Indeed, many of the best teachers are not writers at all. But they do need to be able to communicate clearly with their audiences, and they do need to be able to recognize the literary genre and limitations within the Bible and convey that knowledge to their audiences. Understanding literary style, customs, and conventions is a must if you are an interpreter of the greatest piece of literature ever written—the Bible.

His name was Christopher Armitage, with degrees from Oxford no less, and he taught English literature at Carolina. Indeed, the "venerable Armitage" still teaches English literature at Carolina, forty years later than when I had the man! Even my daughter got to take Shakespeare with him in a summer Oxford program. I had decided to take a degree in English literature at Carolina after having been in pre-med, then political science, then philosophy, then religion ... you get the picture. One semester I was majoring in one subject, the next semester I found something I liked better. I finally settled on English literature.

And I took a lot of English literature courses (some Russian literature as well). In fact, when I got up to thirteen English lit classes, the department gently suggested I needed to get a life and take some other subjects as well. I can tell you, however, that taking classes in the metaphysical poets, Shakespeare, Chaucer, and so many others has helped me to understand the Bible. After all, the Bible I grew up with was written in Shakespearean English! Indeed, the Bible is the greatest work of literature ever to appear in the English language.

This means that you had better know something about English literature and the Bible's influence on it. A good place to start is by studying William Tyndale and his translation of the Bible. Many of the familiar "biblical" idioms, such as "he escaped by the skin of his teeth," were coined by Tyndale and recycled in the KJV. This also means you had better know the various genres of biblical literature inside and out. You are inevitably going to have questions from pedantic or literalistic readers of the Bible with no literary sensitivity who will ask questions like, "Does God really have fingers, because it says in Psalm 8 the stars are the works of his fingers?" Or how about, "Are the parables descriptions of agricultural and economic realities in Jesus' day?" Or even, "Did God really create the universe in six twenty-four-hour days, and if so, how come he didn't create the sun in our galaxy on the first day?"

In other words, many of the questions people will ask the Bible teacher or scholar are based on an incomprehension of what kind of literature they are reading and what sort of information they can reasonably expect out of that literature. Let me give you a good example.

The Bible as Literature — Ancient Literature

When I was just completing seminary in 1977, a book came out called *The Battle for the Bible* by Harold Lindsell, who at the time was on the Board of Trustees for my seminary — Gordon-Conwell Seminary in Massachusetts. Harold, it must be said, was not really a Bible scholar; indeed, if he had an area of expertise, it seems to have been church history. In this book Lindsell tries to reconcile the several accounts of Peter's denials of Christ, followed by the cock crowing. He reads these accounts as if he were reading works of modern historiography, works characterized by chronological precision. Unfortunately, this is an anachronistic way of reading the Bible, because ancient literary and historical conventions were different from our modern ones. Because of the differences in the accounts of Peter's denials of Christ and the timing and number of the cock crows, Lindsell finally determined that Peter denied Christ six times. Only so could Lindsell completely harmonize in a modern way the four accounts of this story.

But in fact *no gospel says that Peter denied Christ six times, and these four accounts originally were written to four different audiences who would not likely have known about the other accounts.* The first time there was a collection of the four canonical Gospels together in one codex seems to have been in the second century AD. This sort of harmonizing of accounts reflects assumptions about a collected canon and about the historical origins and literary conventions of these books that are not true.

Ancient historians and biographers were perfectly comfortable with giving general rather than specific chronological information when it came to the relating of A to B. All four canonical Gospels agree that Peter denied Jesus three times, and there is agreement that somewhere in or after the process a cock crowed. We must allow these accounts to be imprecise if the authors were not trying to be precise. For Lindsell, this compromised the historical integrity and inerrancy of these accounts. In fact, it does no such thing. What counts as an error must be judged on the basis of what the author was attempting to do, not according to contemporary standards of reporting or of what constitutes an error! If a gospel writer wants to speak in a general way when it comes to chronological matters, we must let him do so.

Let's take one more example of this sort of lack of historical and literary sensitivity. In some places in the Gospels we read that the Son of Man will be killed and after three days rise; in other places we read that he will be killed and on the third day rise. Modern persons will be prone to ask: Which is it? Must there be three twenty-four four days that go by before Jesus can rise, according to the prophecy? The answer is no. Why not? Because the phrase "after three days" often meant in antiquity "after a while." It was not a precise chronological phrase. The more precise phrase is "on the third day." Having some literary understanding of how ancient documents were written, especially when it comes to chronological matters, is crucial to understanding the Bible.

One thing that becomes increasingly clear is that a literary understanding of the Bible and literary sensitivity come only from actually reading and studying literature. In the case of the Bible this means ancient Near Eastern literature, early Jewish literature, Greco-Roman literature, and early Christian literature. The reason is obvious—you begin to see the patterns in the different genres of literature. For example, if you read a variety of the early Jewish apocalypses, you begin to understand how a text like Daniel or Revelation was intended to work, as well as what sort of information you can and cannot expect to extract from it.

Or again, if you study both ancient letters and ancient rhetoric, you will discover that: (1) the so-called letters in the New Testament are in some cases not letters at all, but rather sermons (e.g., 1 John), and in some cases they are more treatises or discourses than they are like ancient letters (e.g., Romans), and (2) many of them owe more to rhetorical conventions than to epistolary ones, especially if we are talking about the bulk of the document between the epistolary opening and closing elements. But you would never know this unless you studied both ancient letters and ancient rhetoric. The literary genre and context are crucial to understanding the text. Furthermore, there are social conventions that are in play and are used in rhetorical fashion to make a point.

Rhetorical Conventions or Apostolic Hubris?

Let's consider an example of socio-rhetorical conventions. What in the world is going on in 2 Corinthians 10–13, especially considering what Paul says in 1 Corinthians 1 that he will boast in nothing but the cross of Christ? Isn't he boasting about himself in 2 Corinthians 10–13 (or in Phil. 3)? What should we make of Paul's autobiographical remarks in such texts?

As it turns out, there were rhetorical rules about boasting. In fact Plutarch wrote a little treatise on what constituted "Inoffensive Self Praise." What is interesting about 2 Corinthians 10–13 is that while Paul does follow these rules in a self-deprecating sort of way, he also subverts the whole way that ancients would normally boast about themselves by boasting of things they would never brag about. No one would brag about how many times they had been stoned, how many times they had been run out of town, how many times they had been shipwrecked, and how many times they had been pursued and betrayed by their co-religionists, and especially no one would have bragged about how they escaped danger by being lowered over a city wall in a basket under the cover of darkness. I like to call this story (mentioned in both Acts 9:25 and 2 Cor. 11:32–33) St. Paul the Basket Case.

There is profound irony in this story because in the Roman military, there was an award called the Wall Crown, given to the soldier who was the first bravely to scale a city wall and help capture a besieged city. Paul is bragging about exactly the opposite. He says in effect, "I was first down the wall, in a basket, escaping danger under cover of darkness." I find it interesting that Paul can both use the rhetorical conventions and at the same time subvert the normal way they would be used by doing mock boasting or boasting in things that no normal, sane, first-century person would boast about. On top of all of this, Paul is also inverting the way the ancients viewed honor and shame. He is "glorying in his shame," to use an oxymoron.

If you are going to understand the New Testament, one must learn to think along with its authors, which among other things involves thinking theologically and ethically. It's not enough to have linguistic, historical, archaeological, or even literary sensitivity if the goal is understanding, teaching, or even writing about the substance of the New Testament. In the next chapter we must deal with the theology and ethics of the New Testament and how one prepares to teach and write about it. In preparation for that, here is a little meditation on the interface between simple objects like a cup and profound theological reflection.

BLOOD VESSELS

"In Principio erat Verbum"

Chalice, Cup
Grail, Goblet
Waiting Wine Glass—
Blood Vessels.

Plate, Patin
Wafer, Morsel
Beckoning Bread Basket—
Table Service.

Mere morsels
Or Bare Body?
Uncommon Cup
Or Challenging Chalice?

From Sacrifice
To Sacrament
From Sign to Symbol
From Servant to Service
Grace Comes a Calling.

Blood Shed
Blood Transfusion
His Extinction
Our Distinction
By Intinction.

"You are what you Eat."

BW III
Fall, 2004

6

SUMMA THEOLOGICA:
KNOWING YOUR THEOLOGY AND ETHICS

Learning to Think Logically and Theologically

I was teaching Sunday school in Durham, England, at Elvet Methodist Church. It was the Christmas season, so naturally the subject at hand was the birth narratives. A bright girl named Rachel, who was about seven at the time, came up to me after class and asked the following: "So, if God is Jesus' Father and Mary is Jesus' mother, are God and Mary married? And if not ... [dramatic pause and with some hesitation] ... is he illegitimate?" Honestly, this was a better theological question than I often get in seminary classes these days. Rachel had already begun the pilgrimage of learning how to think logically and theologically at the same time about Bible stories. It is an art I wished more students had these days.

Part of the problem is that in recent decades there has been considerable pushback against theological readings of the Bible. Some, in the school and service of social scientific interpretation of the Bible, have tried to avoid theological readings of the Bible, as if the Bible could be reduced to a pile of social conventions, archaeological realia, and cultural artifacts. While the Bible certainly involves such things, at the end of the day the theological and ethical substance of the Bible cannot be ignored, nor should its importance be minimized or trivialized.[6] But how does one learn to think theologically?

---

6. Of late there has been a reaction to this sort of reductionism, leading to several series of theological commentaries on the Bible.

When I was in seminary, we were required to read a helpful little book by Helmut Thielicke entitled *A Little Exercise for Young Theologians*. The book is only fifty-six pages long, translated from German, and it is still in print and in demand decades after I first read the book, precisely because it is full of wisdom. One element this book cautions is doing theology that goes beyond what is written in the Bible, especially when one is inventing ideas that are not even consonant with the Bible — for example, the idea that the Bible teaches us that Jesus was a sinner like the rest of us, or else he could never have fully identified with us. These sorts of ideas and assumptions reflect a lack of good theological training of the mind, that is, to think in ways that are consonant with the Scriptures. The author of Hebrews, for example, tells us explicitly that Jesus was tempted like us in every respect, except he never sinned.

Thielicke rightly urges his audience to rise to the challenge of dealing with difficult and complex theological and ethical ideas and concepts in the Bible. The mind must be teased into active theological thought. One must begin to grapple with ideas like the virginal conception and bodily resurrection of Jesus, the deity of Christ, the personhood of the Holy Spirit, the inspiration and authority of the Bible, the concept of sin (original and ordinary), or the nature of God (all-seeing, all-powerful, all-loving, etc.). One must also come to grips with ethical concepts like the fallenness of humankind, the role of commandments in the Christian life, the imitation of Christ, the ways in which we are created and renewed in God's image, and what the Bible says about a whole host of moral topics (sexual ethics, money, justice, work, etc.). It is impossible to understand, teach, or write about the Bible meaningfully if you do not have a basic grasp of its theological and ethical content.

Thinking with the Authors

Perhaps the first essential step to the goal of becoming a young theologian or ethicist is enlarging your vocabulary. Both New Testament theology and New Testament ethics, like many specialized fields of study, have a specialized vocabulary. Terms like paraenesis, virginal conception, and original sin need to be learned. The way into understanding theological and ethical concepts is in part through learning the meaning of key terms.

The second step in the process is learning how to think as the New Testament writers thought. For example, Paul in 1 Corinthians 15:13–15 tells us that "if there is no resurrection of the dead, then not even Christ has been raised. And if Christ has not been raised, our preaching is useless and so is your faith. More than that, we are then found to be false witnesses about God, for we have testified about God that he raised Christ from the dead." What sort of syllogistic logic is this? It is, of course, a logic that does not involve just abstract thinking, but is also a reflection on historical events and their theological and ethical implications.

Despite the tendency of some to suggest that being a person of faith means you should *not* learn to think critically about the Bible or your faith, in fact the Bible demands that we learn to think with discernment, to reason about what the Bible says, and even to be able to give a reason for the hope that is within us (1 Peter 3:15). Critical thinking is not only not at odds with biblical faith; it is required to have a rudimentary understanding of the theology and ethics that are part of the substance of that faith.

Just a Thought? Faith in Faith?

One of the dangers in entering the theological or ethical playground is that you might think you are dealing merely with ideas—ideas that can be debated, batted around, shaped, and reshaped. But in fact the writers of the New Testament are not merely encouraging us to enter a debating club where ideas are thrown around like Frisbees. The New Testament writers believe they are talking about realities—real persons like Jesus, real events like the resurrection, real experiences like the new birth. The moment theological or ethical reflection forgets that ideas are ways of talking about such realities is the moment when one has untethered theological or ethical discussion from its historical or real foundation.[7] There is always a

---

7. I would distinguish between what is historically real (e.g., the resurrection of Jesus), and the larger category of reality (e.g., God the Father is one, but at the same time that oneness is expressed in three persons, three personal expressions: Father, Son, and Holy Spirit).

danger when theology or ethics are disconnected from the storied world in which they are grounded and the symbolic universe that undergirds it. For example, the virginal conception is not just an idea—it is an event that happened in the life of a young Jewish girl named Mary.

I was once asked if I believed in adult baptism. My response was: "Believe in it? I've seen it." Similarly Mary, if asked if she believed in the virginal conception, could have responded just as I did about baptism. She experienced the virginal conception. Sometimes we make the mistake of assuming that faith in something is the reality of that something, or even that our faith is what makes that "something" real or makes it happen. This is not so. Faith is not like putting yeast in dough. My faith in the resurrection is not what made Jesus rise from the dead.

The resurrection of Jesus either happened or it didn't. Whether I believe in it or not is a second order question. My faith or trust that Jesus did rise from the dead neither makes it so, nor does it make it more real. It only allows me to have a more personal connection with the risen Jesus and receive some of the benefits that have resulted from his resurrection. That's all. Faith has an object, if we are talking about biblical faith. It is not simply belief in belief or faith in faith. These are precisely the sort of issues you have to begin to sort out when you learn to think theologically and ethically, as the Bible encourages us to do.

The Reading List

I regularly advise my students, if what they want is to become young theologians or ethicists, they should not just to read the Bible but also read classic works on the Bible that do indeed think theologically and ethically about the Bible. For example, read some of John Chrysostom's amazing *Homilies on the Letters of Paul*. Or read Augustine's *The City of God*, Thomas a Kempis's *The Imitation of Christ*, some of John Calvin's *Institutes* (try the section on the Holy Spirit). Or read J. I. Packer's *Knowing God*, or D. Bonhoeffer's *The Cost of Discipleship*, or C. S. Lewis's *Mere Christianity*. I could go on and on with this bibliography.

My forebear John Wesley had a considerable list that he expected his preachers to read if they were to be good preachers who thought theologically and ethically, and he said much about the importance of reading—and he was talking to *preachers*. One can only imagine what he would have said to those aspiring to *teach* the Bible or be a Bible scholar. Here is part of a letter written to John Premboth on August 17, 1760:

> What has exceedingly hurt you in time past, nay, and I fear to this day, is want of reading. I scarce ever knew a preacher read so little. And perhaps, by neglecting it, you have lost the taste for it. Hence your talent in preaching does not increase. It is just the same as it was seven years ago. It is lively, but not deep; there is little variety, there is no compass of thought. Reading only can supply this, with meditation and daily prayer. You wrong yourself greatly by omitting this. You can never be a deep preacher without it, any more than a thorough Christian. O begin! Fix some part of every day for private exercises. You may acquire the taste which you have not: what is tedious at first, will afterwards be pleasant. Whether you like it or no, read and pray daily. It is for your life; there is no other way; else you will be a trifler all your days, and a petty, superficial preacher. Do justice to your own soul; give it time and means to grow. Do not starve yourself any longer. Take up your cross and be a Christian altogether. Then will all children of God rejoice (not grieve) over you in particular.

As for what John Wesley set forth as a library for a preacher, just reading the table of contents of the thirty-volume set he published under the title "A Christian Library" takes one's breath away. Wesley himself set about to edit a series of classic Christian works for his preachers and expected preachers to read excerpted portions from hundreds of Christian classics.[8]

John Wesley calls this "extracts of practical divinity," and there is as much emphasis on ethics and praxis as there is on theology proper. Wesley selected from some ancient sources, but mostly he chose works originally published in English, and mostly from

---

8. See the list in Appendix 2.

Anglican and Puritan divines. It is noteworthy as well that he used extracts from works written by Calvinists such as John Owen, Richard Baxter, or Jonathan Edwards, not just from works by Arminians of one sort or another. He wanted his preachers to read broadly in "practical divinity."

This is my advice as well. Don't just read academic and abstract works of theology and ethics. Read things that will improve your Christian character and walk with Christ. If you are going to be a Bible teacher, a Bible scholar, a theologian, or an ethicist, you should be exhibiting a Christlike character, not just an encyclopedic knowledge of the Bible or your subject matter.

What happens when you read good theological or ethical books is the same thing that happens when you begin to learn a language. You begin to acquire vocabulary and gain a certain amount of skill and familiarity with the universe of discourse in which you are now orbiting. This, too, is an ongoing part of the equipping of the Bible scholar or Bible teacher.

It is not enough to know the Bible well. Greater minds than ours have reflected on the Bible before we ever thought of doing so, and our reading of the Bible will only be enriched if we read the classic Christian works and so end up reading the Bible with the saints. I like to use the analogy of standing on the shoulders of those who have gone before us. If you picture a human pyramid, there can be no disputing that the person at the top of the pyramid can see further and better than the one standing on the ground. So it is with us if we learn with the saints to read the Bible theologically and ethically.

Cross Disciplinary Training

One of the problems in a world of overspecialization is that we have Christian theologians and ethicists who do their work without any meaningful interaction with Bible scholars. For example, I have seen studies on the ethics of artificial insemination, abortion, or gay marriage that hardly interact with what biblical scholars are thinking about such subjects. Equally, we have exegetical studies on this or that passage of the Bible that hardly ever draw out the theological or ethical implications of such a passage. Not only do we need more dialogue across disciplines, we need more Bible scholars who actually are committed to be biblical theologians and biblical ethicists, seeking to apply the insights they have gained from the Bible to current and pressing theological and ethical issues.

I have been encouraged by the conferences sponsored by St. Andrews University that gather together a group of Bible scholars and theologians to reason about the substance of a particular biblical book (John and Hebrews have been the focus of two of the conferences). My own experience at such a conference is that predictably the exegetes were worried the theologians were reading more into and out of the text than what was there, imposing systematic theological categories on the text; the theologians, by contrast, complained, sometimes rightly, that the exegetes never got beyond the arguing about grammar, syntax, historical and literary context, and the literal meaning of the text. Both of these laments are probably justified, but at least the task of integration was being broached and approached.

One of the things I encourage young Bible teachers and scholars to do is not merely cross-disciplinary reading, but cross-disciplinary teaching and conferencing. By this I mean that one can team-teach a course with an ethicist on the ethics of the New Testament. Or, for example, one can attend a meeting of the Wesleyan Theological Society with the intent of trying to understand better Wesleyan theology in light of the Bible, and vice versa.

In my case, the first teaching I did at the graduate level was teaching the Standard Sermons of John Wesley at Duke Divinity School as an entry into Wesleyan theology. I became authorized to teach Wesleyan history, theology, and polity by my church (the United Methodist Church), and when I finally became a full-time seminary professor at Ashland Theological Seminary, I taught both OT and NT as well as the three Wesleyan courses just mentioned. As you might imagine, this led to considerable integration in my thinking about the separable disciplines of biblical studies and Wesleyan studies.

It would be good for any Bible teacher or scholar to be well-versed in their own faith tradition (be it Calvinistic, Arminian,

Pentecostal, Catholic, or Orthodox) as well as in the Bible, especially if one is going to be teaching mainly people in one's one tradition. Even in an age where denominationalism is breaking down, the theological differences remain, and the theological and ethical traditions continue to have influence on Christian thinking.

It is furthermore a useful exercise to cultivate friendships across the disciplines. If you teach in a college or seminary, start with the colleagues where you work. For my part, I have been blessed to be a part of a movement called the John Wesley Fellows. A Foundation for Theological Education (AFTE) sponsored this movement through scholarships and conferencing, and in the conferencing that happens each Christmas season, all sorts of fertile interactions take place across the disciplines. Young theologians critique young church historians' papers; senior biblical scholars critique young ethicists' papers, and so on. It has been good to be part of this cross-disciplinary fellowship for some thirty-three years now. It has certainly enriched my understanding of the Bible and my ability to teach it. I have also learned a lot about pedagogy in the context of this Fellowship.

Finally, I think one has to be intentional from the outset about the theology and ethics of the Bible. That is, you must commit yourself to serve the church, and this in turn means you have to be prepared to answer the questions laypeople and young college and seminary students are asking about theology and ethics—practical questions, profound questions, introductory questions, and questions of praxis. This requires a commitment to a thoroughgoing processing of what one learns from the Bible so that you can articulate its theological and ethical implications and applications to any level of audience. Eventually the ethics and the theology of the Bible will catch up with you if you are a practicing Christian and especially a minister.

On Being a Global Christian

In a twenty-first-century world, so interwoven as it is in a global economy, it seems clear that I need to be a global Christian, not just an American one; I must be concerned about and be serving the church around the world. If you have the privilege of teaching and preaching abroad, take full advantage of those opportunities. Cross-cultural experiences will enrich your teaching and your Christian life and make you far less of a parochial person.

Paul told us all along that in Christ, there is neither Jew nor Gentile, neither American nor Chinese, for all are one in Christ. We must implement the implications of such a spiritual reality. If this means sacrificing some of our national ideas and national identity in order to be a world Christian and have a worldwide ministry of Bible teaching—so be it. Our Christian identity should be our primary identity, and our solidarity with other Christians everywhere should be our main concern. The Bible is for everyone, and that has implications for Bible teachers and scholars and how they view themselves and their service to the Lord and his church around the world.

Honesty Is the Best Policy

I was minding my own business one day in my office when a knock came on my door. It was one of my former students, whom I had not seen in some years. He had graduated from seminary and was doing ministry somewhere in the Midwest. He had to remind me of his name, as it had been quite a while, and I have been teaching for close to thirty years now. I asked him to come in and sit down, figuring he just wanted to catch up and maybe reminisce a bit or ask some advice. In fact, he became quite agitated and nervous, struggling with what he was about to say. What finally came out of his mouth was that he had cheated on one of the exams he had taken for one of my courses. It had been a take home exam and was supposed to be an open brain, but not an open book exam, taken on the honor system. Unfortunately, he had succumbed to using various resources in order to procure a good grade on the test.

As you might imagine, I was saddened by this conversation. He told me, "I am willing to take whatever consequences you deem appropriate at this juncture." The man clearly had a guilty conscience; as he admitted, he had been fretting over this sin for a long time. While I could have told him that I would have to go to the administration and have his degree temporarily revoked until he redid the class in an honest manner (it was, after all, a required class), I realized this would have had serious consequences for his ongoing ministry, his ability to support his family, and a host of other considerations. I decided that the better part of wisdom was to forgive him, but to insist that he make sure going forward that he "go and sin no more."

Honesty is indeed something close akin to truth. You cannot be a good advocate for Truth with a capital T if your own personal honesty doesn't bear close scrutiny. I told this pastor that now that this ethical weakness had surfaced in his life, it would be good for him to have in place some accountability structures for his ministry, so that more ethical problems might not arise when the heat of the moment got red hot.

The life of the Bible teacher or scholar, if done in the context of Christian ministry or just a normal Christian life, will indeed involve from time to time doing some pastoral counseling, advising, and correcting on the basis of what you yourself have learned from the Bible's theology and ethics. Indeed, such moments as the one just mentioned are where the rubber meets the road, where your belief and teaching are tested in the fiery kiln of praxis and day-to-day Christian living and behavior. There needs to be not merely *integration* between one's Bible knowledge and theology and ethics; there must also be *integrity* — ethical and theological integrity in one's own life — and a witnessing to others about the need for such integrity in any Christian life, let alone the life of a minister. This is something we all must wrestle with. It's one thing to teach the ethics and theology of the Bible; it's another thing to live it.

One of my favorite quotes from Chaucer's *Canterbury Tales* is found in the Prologue, where we read: "If gold rusts, what then will iron do? For if a priest be foul, on whom we trust, No wonder that a common man should rust." In other words, the teacher or scholar of God's Word needs to be a biblical example to those whom he or she teaches. As James 3:1 reminds us, God holds teachers to a higher standard of rectitude than others. This is another way of saying that a Bible teacher or scholar ought to live out the theology and ethics he has imbibed from the detailed study of the Word. He or she must be a good witness, a living witness. To whom more is given, more is required.

Put another way, it is not enough to know the Bible if you want to teach it. You need to know the God of the Bible. Furthermore, you need to be able to articulate your faith in both the written and the living Word of God in theologically and ethically fruitful ways that will lead others in the paths of righteousness for his name's sake. It is a high calling, a challenging calling, and since it is true for better or worse that your pupils will imitate you if they admire you, you had best get on with imitating Christ and integrating your knowledge and vital piety, day by day.

PURITY

Purity came down from above
Silently, painfully slow
"Though your sins be as red as scarlet
I'll wash them white as snow."

A gift of unfailing love
That chills one to the bone
Sinking in crevasses deep,
Not leaving unturned one stone.

A pure and penetrating cold
Wind piercing between soul and spirit
As if the entire person was needing
To experience, to feel, and to hear it.

Was needing a complete cleansing
A making of all things new
Not just an external makeover
But an internal spring-cleaning too.

I stood and watched the cold beauty
And felt it with some alarm
I wrapped my mantle around me
To shield myself from harm.

But a still small voice whispered
In the silence, I could barely hear
"Open up your heart and being
And let me wash you clear."

I feared I'd be God's frozen person
I feared an unalterable change
I feared no one would know me
I feared I'd be judged strange.

But the snow it just kept falling
An ensign of his constant grace
I unbuttoned my woolen jacket
The flakes fell full on my face.

Purity came down from above
And I chose to let it in
And that has made all the difference,
And yes, I would do it again.

BW III

7

THE WRITE STUFF:
THE ABILITY TO RESEARCH AND WRITE

The Past Is Prologue

I've been a writer of sorts since I was very small. Of course I wrote papers in school. I remember one I wrote in the third grade (age nine). It was on the *Parables of Peanuts*. When I recently went back and read this paper, what amazed me about it is that already I was concerned about people embracing the Christian faith. I said in that little review paper that if more people would read this Charles Schultz book, they might be led to Christ, or words to that effect. I remember as well, during elementary school, passing along little notes of suggestion to poor Dr. Huggins, my Methodist minister, with suggestions on what he might consider preaching on! More importantly, I remember writing poetry, quite a lot of it, from an early age. I loved the spoken and written word.

In the sixth grade our ambitious young teacher Mr. Poindexter announced that our class would perform Shakespeare's *Macbeth* before the PTA and the whole school, and would someone please volunteer to play the role of the lead bad guy—Macbeth. I raised my hand immediately and proceeded to begin to memorize my lines that very night. The play went off without a hitch before the PTA—until the young man playing Macduff, the hero, after having dispatched me with a sword and standing over my prone form, said, "There lies the dead Macduff" (instead of Macbeth). It was probably the first time ever that the climax of *Macbeth* produced considerable laughter from the audience.

I saw then already the connection between good (and correct) speaking and good writing, between good reading and good writing, between learning and researching, and teaching and even preaching. It was all interrelated.

There are telltale signs in a person's life as to whether they are cut out to be good writers or not. For one thing, you learn a lot about yourself during the dissertation phase of your doctoral work. If writing that dissertation is like pulling teeth without anesthesia, if it's a difficult process requiring endless correction and revision, and drafting and redrafting, it is probably a sign of things to come. I have even known two people who have had a terminal case of thesis. One took seventeen years to finish his degree at Harvard; the other is amazingly still in process some thirty years down the road!

I am not talking here merely about the uncertainties one may feel or the sense of being overwhelmed that one may feel in the process of writing a doctoral dissertation. Nor am I merely referring to the paralysis of overanalysis that does happen as well, which can stop a thesis dead in its tracks. These are all psychological factors that may affect whether one ever finishes a degree.

I am mainly here referring to what you can learn about whether you have the gift of writing during the production of the doctoral thesis. Some people never get beyond the writing and publishing of the dissertation, and in some cases this is a good thing, because they probably don't have a gift for writing. Moreover, the sort of written work they produce is such that even scholars find it hard going to read and glean insights from. Some writers of dissertations would even put their own mothers or fathers to sleep, since they have written so tediously, turgidly, or technically, or frankly just poorly.

Therein lies a further problem. There are many dissertations that never get published, even some pretty good ones. Some scholars resort to self-publishing, which the guild recognizes for what it is—the proof that the peer reviews of the document were probably not promising enough to induce a real publisher to put the thesis into print. This is not always true, of course. Because the new scholar is unknown to most of his or her audience in the guild, publishers often will not take a manuscript simply because they don't think it will sell sufficiently. It may say nothing about the quality of the thesis or the quality of the writing.

Ars Longa, Vita Brevis

The lifeblood of a good scholar is, of course, good researching, and then conveying what he or she has learned through good writing and giving good lectures based on the research. The delivery of the content of the research can be done at many different levels, of course. In my case, while I was and am happy on occasion to deliver purely academic lectures, when it came to most of my publishing, I felt I should try to reach a broader audience—not just scholars, but teachers, educated laypeople, and students (both college and seminary students).

It has become especially apparent to me over the course of the last fifteen years that my books have taken on a life of their own, in part because I wrote mostly for an audience broader than just the guild of scholars. My books have a ministry of their own, quite apart from whatever I am currently doing. They minister to people I have never met, and in some cases, never will meet.

My teaching and preaching around the world (I've been all over North America, Europe, the Middle East, South Africa, Zimbabwe, Singapore, Hong Kong, Australia, and New Zealand) have only had a fraction of the impact of my books, and my personal impact is much more temporary and transitory. In fact, the main thing that has prompted the invitation to teach and preach all over the world is my books, which have been read in all these places and more.

I received a letter the other day from a student at a seminary in Addis Ababa, Ethiopia. It was followed by a letter from a student on the north coast of Turkey. Both were requesting books from me; yet they don't know me and have never met me. But they know my books. This approach has led to the sale of close to a half million books. I don't say this to boast but to demonstrate that if you write for a broader audience, and if you have the gift of writing for these sorts of audiences, the impact of your scholarship can be considerable and worldwide; it can open doors for you to share the good news with many more people.

The question is: What sort of scholar do you want to be? Do you want to be a scholar who is mainly capable of talking to other scholars in your field? Or do you feel called to a broader ministry, writing for laypeople and students as well as scholars? I have personally tried to engage at all three levels of writing, but it takes skill to write with clarity at all levels of discourse. Blessed are those who know both the possibilities and the limitations of their writing gifts and calling.

Obviously, a young scholar will need to write at a high academic level in order to gain promotion and tenure in the institution in which he or she teaches, and this can be a problem. Indeed, if I were teaching mainly in secular universities, a good deal of my publishing would *not* be viewed as "serious scholarly work," even though such an evaluation would be wrong and unfair—and frankly pejorative. In other words, a young scholar must understand clearly what sort of academic institution she teaches in, in the early stages of her publishing career. I have known situations where a person was denied tenure not because he had not done some "serious academic publishing," but because he had *also* done more popular level writing.

When, however, a Christian scholar finds himself or herself in a situation like this, one still must ask the question: "What would the Lord have me do, and what sort of writing ministry am I called to?" and not merely the question: "How can I best feather my academic nest in my present setting?" Sometimes conservative Christian scholars get jobs in institutions where the very calling on their life to the ministry of being a Bible teacher or Bible scholar may be seriously compromised if they simply comply with the wishes and demands of a secular institution when it comes to gaining promotion and tenure.

And there is another pitfall to look out for as well—namely, yourself.

Coeur in Curvatus in Se?

What I mean by the above phrase is that persons who go through all the rigors of education and training that it takes to become a teacher or a scholar inevitably tend to evaluate themselves on the basis of how other teachers and scholars evaluate them. They long for the encouragement and approval of others, which gives them confidence they are on the right track. This is both natural and human. The problem comes, however, when one deliberately begins to play to the crowd, play to the human audience one most wants the approval of, and in the process ignores, sublimates, or even denies the calling of God on their life in terms of the sort of writing they have been gifted and called to do.

I have seen young Christian scholars, striving so hard to be recognized not merely in their school but in their guild, that they completely lose focus on what led them to pursue such a calling in the first place. Sadly, I have even seen young conservative scholars largely give up their orthodox faith in order to be better accepted by other scholars and colleagues whom they admire. You need to ask the question: *Am I primarily playing to an audience of One, or to an audience of many?* And sometimes even when a person is mainly playing to an audience of one, it needs to be asked, which one? Yourself? Your mother? Your mentor? Or God? Whom do you most seek to please or honor, or of whom do you seek the approval? These are the sort of personal questions you as a Christian teacher or scholar, and especially a young one, need to ask yourself regularly.

Unfortunately, we live in a culture of "experts" where expertise is revered; sadly, people's egos get bound up in the desire to be a "world's leading authority in X." The expert too often feels it is enough to do pure research. He has no need to distill things for the masses; that's beneath his dignity and pay scale. It is enough to live in one's head and to talk only to other equally heady folk in the same field.

Whatever the merits of this approach to research in other fields, a Christian who is a Bible teacher or scholar should never take such an approach. Never! Research by a Christian is never done just for its own sake, or even just to advance knowledge in a given field. It is done in service to the Lord *and to his church*. I must confess I am sometimes baffled by some Christian NT scholars who are perfectly content to just talk to small circles of like-minded experts without any sense of responsibility to share their knowledge with a broader audience—indeed with the church.

Broadening Your Horizons, Honing Your Craft

One thing that helps learning how to write to various audiences is speaking to various audiences. If you regularly have to teach Sunday school classes or Bible studies or preach to congregations, you are regularly engaged in the art of trying to speak with clarity to the broadest possible audience. Here is an important point that needs to be reiterated—you need to boil it up, before you boil it down. That is, you need to have done the hard work of research and study before you teach or preach the Word. One of the reasons I have written commentaries on every book of the NT is to help me know enough to be able to teach those books, learning what the state of the discipline is on those books. Good research doesn't necessarily lead to good writing, but it certainly should lead to good teaching.

There are certain skills one can acquire to become a better, if not a good researcher and writer. First, you need to have a love for learning and a commitment to lifelong learning. It is this love for learning that keeps you at a difficult research task day in and day out, until you wrestle a blessing out of the data—indeed, until you wrestle some insight out of the mass of data. Without such a love, researching and writing up the results of the research become an onerous task.

Second, even if writing is not your main gift, you can improve your writing skills simply by doing it. It's like riding a bicycle. The more you practice, the better you get at it. This is especially true if you let someone who is good at grammar, syntax, vocabulary, and style read what you write and serve as an informal editor. I have had many professional editors at publishing houses, but I also have had my wife read things I write, in order to edit and critique them. If that is a little too close to the bone and creates problems for you, have a trusted friend make suggestions about style and content. You need to have feedback if you want to become a better writer.

Becoming a better researcher requires a different skill set than becoming a better writer. There are plenty of good writers who don't have much to say, and this includes people in the area of biblical studies. Becoming a better researcher requires going to the places where you can best do primary source research. This will usually require travel. No, you can't simply rely on the stuff available online or on the Internet. The problem with the Internet is it makes us all lazy. We begin to believe we can find anything on the Internet if we are just computer and web savvy enough. This is false. You can waste a lot of time searching for things on the Internet, when what is needed is to travel to an actual library or consult with scholars in person.

Without question a prerequisite to becoming a better researcher is being able to work with the three major research languages — English, French, and German. I was once the external examiner for a thesis written in Singapore. As I read the thesis, which had some merit, I discovered that the doctoral candidate had done little or no research in German of the relevant NT scholarship in that language. I wrote the dean back and asked him if he found this an acceptable practice. His answer, sadly, was yes. It should have been no. Anyone wanting to be a good scholar has to deal with the primary and secondary sources in various languages. Period. Exclamation point!

There are some acquired skills that can help make research less onerous and time consuming. For example, there are shortcuts. You should start by reading through *New Testament Abstracts* and its English summaries of articles, monographs, and commentaries. You should look for seminal articles, monographs, and commentaries and read the footnotes carefully to see what sources these writers consulted. One should concentrate on the major NT journals everyone is expected to read: *Novum Testamentum (NovT)*, *New Testament Studies (NTS)*, *Journal for Biblical Literature (JBL)*, *Zeitschrift für die neutestamentliche Wissenschaft (ZNW)*, to name but four. You should start by reading those who have labored long in the Pauline vineyard or the Johannine vineyard and who are experts in these areas. They will survey the landscape for you and help you figure out quickly the most helpful resources.

How to Read and Learn Wisely

When you are reading a detailed article, monograph, or commentary, read the summaries and conclusions first, to see where the writer is going. Then concentrate on the portions of the books or articles that are most directly germane to your interest and subject. This will save you a lot of time poring through endless data hoping to find something helpful. Develop a note-taking or underlining practice that helps you highlight the main ideas or key quotes you will want to use later.

Word to the wise: Kindle can't really help you if you want to do the sort of research I am talking about, because you need to be able to go back and forth in a book easily and find the places you have highlighted or where you have written marginal notes. In my case this is especially crucial, as I have something of a photographic memory—though as my wife reminds me, some of the film is overexposed and some underdeveloped. By this I mean when I read something carefully using my underlining and starring and bracketing and marginalia system, I then fix the image of that page in my brain and I can easily find it later while writing a book. This is a form of actually learning what you are reading. It is one thing to read and understand. It is another thing to read, understand, and learn, and even memorize.

Unfortunately in an Internet age, the computer disables one's oral memory and provides a disincentive to memorizing things. I should hasten to add, however, that the computer also makes writing and editing much less difficult and time consuming than it used to be. Back B.C. (Before Computers), my poor wife had to type my doctoral thesis three times on an IBM Selectric typewriter, changing font balls from English, to Greek, to Hebrew. I wouldn't wish that on anyone these days. The value of being a B.C. person is that you see both the advantages and the drawbacks to using computers for research and writing.

Publish or Perish?

One day, I was having a good chat with my friend Richard Hays about writing. He was exhorting me to write less and ponder more, whereas I was urging him to ponder less (lest he become ponderous) and write more. We need more from his pen. By the time we had this conversation, I had written quite a few books— not just articles, but books. In fact, there was a standing joke about me (which also circulated about Tom Wright). The joke was that a student called Asbury asking to speak to me. The secretary told him I was busy writing a book. The student succinctly replied, "That's fine. I'll hold."

If a seminary or Christian college has a wise provost or dean or department chair, he or she will realize that they need some faculty who are master teachers but publish little, and some scholars who can both teach and publish, and some who would be better just being research professors. It takes a variety of faculty to make up a good school. But alas, even in schools that have such administrators, promotion and sabbaticals are often based on publications or planned publications, not just on reviews of one's classroom performances. Thus, some scholars who find research and writing a huge cross to bear are forced to carry that cross all the way to Golgotha Publishing House in order to get promoted. It really ought not to be that way at a Christian school, where the main goal should be "training students or budding clergy in the way that they should go."

Sometimes and in some institutions, the pressure for a Bible scholar to publish is immense. We've all heard the cry, "Publish or perish." There are alternatives. One can publish and parish as I did in the first four years after my dissertation. While I was busy pastoring four Methodist churches, I published various scholarly articles, got my dissertation published in two parts, and wrote a monthly column for the *North Carolina Christian Advocate*. But it wasn't what I had published, it was who I was and what I could teach that got me my first full-time academic job at an evangelical seminary in Ashland, Ohio.

Sometimes, of course, you can put pen to paper too quickly, and then later regret what you wrote as something not perfected or profound or edited enough. Sometimes, however, you have to strike while the iron is hot, if the goal is an urgent ministry need. I remember Jim Hoover of InterVarsity Press contacting me about quickly writing a response book to the *Da Vinci Code*. I said sure, and in about three weeks time I had written *The Gospel Code*. There are a number of reasons why this was possible: (1) it was January when I wasn't teaching; (2) I already knew the subject matter and had read the novel by Dan Brown; (3) I didn't have to do any additional research for this particular book, just put pen to paper; and (4) this sort of popular level book is easier for me to write. Besides, I was deeply concerned about the impact Brown's novel was having, and so I had a sense of calling and urgency about responding to it.

Write on Cue

I have often been asked how I am able to write so much. Is sleep optional, I was once asked? Let me first just say that I go to bed at 11:00 every night, or a little before, and I get up about 6:15 to 6:30 every morning when I am in my normal routine. On weekdays when I don't lecture at 8 a.m. (namely Monday, Wednesday and Friday), I tend to go jogging or walk nine holes of golf, carrying my clubs. The latter at this point is more strenuous activity than the former. To do what I do, with fifteen or so off campus events a year, and international travel to teach or preach or do archaeological research almost every summer, it is imperative that I stay in reasonable shape. Gone are my days of running marathons (I ran Cleveland, Boston, and Charlotte in the 1990s). I am but a slow jogger at fifty-nine. But the temple still needs its upkeep, and I try to keep up.

As to writing, I do no writing at the office. When I am at school, I am at school: teaching, meeting with students, going to faculty meetings, going to chapel, eating lunch, or just reading. I do all my writing at home in my comfy chair in the study. I write on a laptop, and yes, I type with just two fingers—but they know where everything is. I write mostly on Mondays and Wednesdays, and on Fridays if I am not heading somewhere to give a lecture or preach.

Another reason I am able to do so many of these things is because our children are grown, and two of them are gainfully employed. The third one is finishing her PhD in philosophy and art and literature at the University of Chicago. We have an empty nest (except for our rambunctious cat) and more time for such things. But I would not be telling you the whole story if I did not tell you more about the sacrifices required to be a biblical scholar, to which we will turn shortly.

Truth Seekers or Novelty Seekers?

Another of the keys to doing good research and writing is to surround yourself with trusted colleagues who can read bits and pieces of what you write and give feedback. Sometimes a scholar will have an idea, find evidence to support the idea, and think it is a good idea, all the while being oblivious to its problems. One of the problems with scholarship in a world where it is assumed that the newest is the truest and the latest is the greatest is that one begins to think that because one has found a new insight, it therefore must be a true insight. Modern scholarship often prizes the new, the innovative, the creative, the unique, and the distinctive, but this should not be the main thrust of biblical scholarship. There should be far more concern with the question "But is it true?" than with the question "What's new?"

To some extent, doctoral programs have helped foster this problem by overstressing that the doctoral thesis needs to offer something "new" to the ongoing discussion. It would be better if such programs simply expected that a good thesis will make some sort of contribution to the ongoing discussion in a given field, not necessarily that it will come up with some *novum*, something radically new.

Scholars seldom think about the issue of "intellectual property rights." There are now whole law firms populated with intellectual property lawyers. In an increasingly litigious world, you need to be careful even when quoting other source material than your own. Few biblical scholars are likely to be guilty of plagiarism — especially, one would hope, believing Christian scholars — but in fact there is more to the intellectual property claims than just concerns about straight plagiarism. One of the reasons for detailed footnotes is to make clear on an ongoing basis one's indebtedness to other scholars' works.

Sometimes, of course, two scholars will nearly simultaneously come up with the same idea, and that can often result in an unseemly turf dispute. For example, the origin of the term "socio-rhetorical" is debated. More than one scholar has claimed to have coined this term or to have some sort of proprietary right to say what this term means, even though no one has, to my knowledge, taken out a copyright on the term. When scholars get into these sorts of turf wars or spitting contests, it is usually unsavory and smacks far too much of hubris. All the same, a researcher and writer must be as careful as possible to give credit where credit is due, by means of footnotes and bibliography. This brings us to our final point in this chapter.

Good bibliography, especially annotated bibliography, helps other scholars do their work, and good footnotes are the breadcrumb trails leading other scholars to viable and valuable resources. Good research and good scholarly writing requires these sorts of apparati, but good popular level writing does not require detailed documentation to the same degree. When it comes to notes and bibliography, remember what sort of document you are writing and for whom.

Even within the varieties of scholarly work, there are levels of discourse. The scholar who is writing about biblical theology, a subject that involves both OT and NT scholars, will want to write at a level that is penetrable for that whole cadre of scholars. In fact, if biblical scholars want historical and systematic theologians to pay attention or even use their work, they need to write using a universe of discourse that such scholars share, to one degree or another. Furthermore, the biblical scholar must have some knowledge of and be savvy about the art of interpretation and the rules of interpretation. Our next port of call must be the subject of hermeneutics. First, however, here is a little meditation about listening not merely to your heart, but to that "still small voice" if it resides within you.

THE SOUND OF THE SOUL

The sound of the soul
At the speed of light
Passed through my brain
And into the night.

Stifling silence
Sensing the sigh
Feeling the longing
Wanting to cry.

The sound of the soul,
Like a getaway train
Doppler effect
Plaintive refrain.

Listening intently
Longing to know
Who am I really?
And does it show?

The sound of the soul
Like a voice in a well
Echoing always
Clear as a bell.

Tuning the instrument
Assessing the tone
Looking for harmony
Searching alone.

Writing it out
To learn what I think
My soul in my words
My brain on the brink.

The sound of the soul
Out of the depths
Heart cry towards heaven
Wordless precepts.

"By him we cry Abba ...
Groaning within
Awaiting adoption
Release from all sin."

"The Spirit assists us
With sighs double deep
Interceding with Abba
My soul to keep."

BW III
January 7, 2006

8

RIGHTLY DIVIDING THE WORD OF TRUTH:
THE ART OF INTERPRETATION AND HERMENEUTICS[9]

Even if you have a vast knowledge of the text of the Bible itself and have memorized large portions of Scripture, there remains the problem of interpretation, especially when you try to relate one Scripture text to another. The Bible is a complex book, and it is frankly too easy to misread some texts in isolation, never mind in combination with other biblical texts. Learning some basic rules of interpretation (*hermeneutics*, as it is called) is essential and separates a merely knowledgeable Bible teacher or scholar from a really good one.

A Wooden Hermeneutic?

When I went to seminary, there was a lot of loose talk about having a wooden hermeneutic. What was usually meant by this phrase was an overly literal way of reading the Bible or a way of proof-texting and sound-byting the Bible that results in the Bible saying things that the inspired authors themselves would be surprised to learn they meant! For example, John of Patmos would have been more than a little surprised to learn he was advocating a flat earth theory when he talked about the angels going to or coming from the four corners of the earth. What the phrase "wooden hermeneutic" too often boiled down to in seminary is one or another

---

9. Some of the material in this chapter appears in another form in my book *The Living Word of God* (Waco, TX: Baylor Univ. Press, 2008).

professor saying, "I wouldn't interpret that text that way." But what one teacher called a wooden hermeneutic turned out to be "rightly dividing the word of truth" in the eyes of another teacher. The rules of the road seemed to vary from driver to driver.

So let us examine some of the tried and true rules for the long and winding road of interpretation of the Bible. But just before we do so, let me tell you a story.

I recently read and reviewed on my blog an interesting and sometimes hilarious book by A. J. Jacobs, *The Year of Living Biblically*.[10] In this book Jacob chronicled how a basically secular Jew tried for 365 days to fulfill literally all the commandments in the OT, in various ways. At one hilarious juncture, he felt he should fulfill the commandment to stone adulterers, but since the text didn't say how large the stones should be, he ended up throwing small pieces of gravel at the persons in question. Even a literal reading of the Bible leaves room for a variety of possible interpretations! So let us consider the rules of the road of Scripture interpretation.

Rule One: *Sola Scriptura*

One of the battle cries of the Reformation was *sola scriptura*. By this was meant that the final authority over the church was the Bible alone. What was not said in this slogan, but was meant, was: the Bible alone, rightly interpreted! Protestants have continued to affirm this principle in one form or another ever since the Reformation. One of the things this principle implied, of course, was that no nonbiblical Christian tradition was immune to revision or critique on the basis of the Bible, no matter how longstanding the tradition.

With the Bible seen as the last court of resort and the litmus test of truth about matters the Word of God spoke to, this in itself set up a kind of suspicion about pneumatic claims. That is, if someone said, "The Spirit told me ..." and what was said was seen as clearly at variance with what the Bible said on that subject, this fresh "revelation" must be critiqued by the canonical

10. A. J. Jacobs, *The Year of Living Biblically* (New York: Simon and Schuster, 2007). My blog can be found most easily at www.benwitherington.com.

one. Sometimes this approach went so far as to suggest that the Holy Spirit no longer spoke independently of God's Word but simply led believers into the truth that was in that Word. Moreover, it meant that while the Spirit could lead persons to say things that went beyond the clear teachings of the Bible, the Spirit that inspired the Scripture itself would *never* lead a person to claim something that contradicts or goes against the text of the Bible. This principle was especially to be put to the test whenever a more pneumatic, charismatic, or experientially oriented revival movement arose within post-Reformation church history. And lest we think that's all a matter of church history, in fact it's happening right now with some of the emerging church movements in 2011.

The tension between the Word and what is thought to be the voice of the Spirit still arises today when some churches or their representatives claim, for example, that God's Spirit has shown that same-sex sexual relationships are not, or are no longer, sinful. Sometimes this hermeneutical move involves arguing that the Bible doesn't say what it appears to have said; but more often, since this move cannot explain away all the biblical data on this matter, the claim is made that new revelation has superseded the old, just as the NT eclipsed various things in the OT.

The living voice of prophecy is appealed to, to justify breaking with traditional exegesis of various biblical passages and ultimately with some parts of the Bible itself. Not surprisingly, evangelicals who have been well schooled in Rule One have largely taken a negative or dim view of these sorts of pneumatic claims since they seem to compromise the authority of the Bible as God's definitive revelation of his will and truth. If rule one really is *sola scriptura,* evangelicals are right to take a dim view of pneumatic claims that go *against* the explicit teaching of the Bible.

Rule Two: Scripture Is Its Own Best Interpreter

One hears a great deal about canonical criticism and canonical theology, which is indeed a manifestation of the old principle that the first and best interpreter of the Bible is the Bible itself. One should compare and contrast various texts within the Bible to gain an understanding of its meaning. What was assumed was that the text was perspicuous, clear in and of itself, and the reader should interpret the more difficult or puzzling passages of the Bible on the basis of the clearer ones. The assumption behind this is that ultimately, there is a single coherent mind behind the entire Bible, and therefore a consistent and coherent revelation within the Bible. What this rule did not take into account is that while the Scripture may be crystal clear, the mind of the modern interpreter at so great a remove in space and time from the writing of the text might be much less than clear.

Part of the problem with this principle is that it sometimes led to a rather flat view of the whole Bible such that levitical laws, for example, were thought to be able to inform the proper interpretation of NT institutions. This, in turn, led to such problematic notions as Sunday being the Sabbath, the Lord's Supper being seen as like the levitical sacrifices, church buildings being seen as temples, and a clerical class being seen as priests. While one can indeed find all of these institutions in the OT, one is hard pressed to find them all imposed on Christians in the NT.

Sometimes this way of interpreting the NT so heavily in light of the OT has led to the elimination of the whole notion that much new is even going on in the NT. The NT is seen rather as the fulfillment or completion, or even the renewal and perfect expression, of the OT. This way of looking at things has especially characterized certain forms of Reformed covenantal theology, and it still does today.

At risk in this sort of approach to the Bible is losing any sense not only of the newness of the new covenant, but of progressive revelation in the Bible. Statements, for example, by Jesus in Mark 10 (about Mosaic legislation being given originally because of the hardness of human hearts but now that the dominion of God is breaking in, new rules apply, and the original creation intent of God before Moses is being reinstated) are either ignored or misinterpreted in the service of preserving one's covenantal theological approach.

This is chiefly a front-to-back approach, by which I mean you start from the front of the Bible and read to the back, and this in turn means that your hermeneutic is so heavily oriented to the OT that by the time you get to the NT, it can hardly be more than just a fulfillment or renewal of the OT. This approach is at variance with the approach of various NT authors, who *begin* with the Christ event and reread the OT in light of the Christ event.

A flat approach to the Bible sometimes also involves the "one covenant but just in various administrations" view. This has been seen by some Protestants as putting the emphasis entirely too strongly on the OT being allowed to determine how the NT can and ought to be understood. Yet there was general agreement that texts like Hebrews, and especially Hebrews 1:1 – 4, established with clarity that Christ and the revelation of God in Christ must be seen as the climax of the revelation of God's truth and Word. If one is thinking narratologically, then a story must be read in light of its climax, and this changes not only what comes thereafter but also how one views what came before the climax.

There was and is enormous debate about how much of the OT is still binding on Christians. One hermeneutical move suggested that the entire OT is still directly binding on Christians except for the portions that are said in the NT to be fulfilled, abrogated, or superseded. The other major hermeneutical move, which caused far fewer difficulties in terms of Christian practice, is the suggestion that only those portions of the OT Law that are reaffirmed in the NT explicitly are binding on Christians. This meant, for example, that since nowhere in the NT are Christians said to be required to observe the Sabbath—indeed there are texts that warn against being trapped into such practices (e.g., Col. 2:16)—that this is no longer an obligation for Christians. For the most part, some form of this second hermeneutical suggestion about the relationship of Christians to obeying OT principles has been accepted and practiced by most Protestants.

Rule Three: The Analogy of Faith

One of the more dominant principles of interpretation in Protestantism is the idea that there is a central theme in Scripture, the great theme of God's divine saving activity, which runs like a red thread right through Scripture. This theme is viewed as a norm so powerful that it has led to the suggestion that if there was a passage of Scripture that seemed at odds with this central theme, someone was obviously misunderstanding the message of that problematic passage.

The phrase *analogia fidei*, "the analogy of faith," in fact comes from the rendering of Romans 12:3 into Latin, but in fact this probably involves a rather clear misinterpretation of the meaning of that verse, which should be compared to Romans 12:6. The proper translation should likely be "according to the measure of faith." Prophets should prophesy, teachers should teach, leaders should lead according to the measure of their current faith, and not beyond it.[11] In other words, this passage has to do with a limitation, but it does not attempt to provide a hermeneutical rule by which one can measure the interpretation of difficult passages or provide a central thematic norm to guide one in the interpretation of such difficult texts. To the contrary, it is about limiting other ministerial activities. Scriptural interpretation is never mentioned here according to the measure or quantity of one's faith, whether great or small.

The Reformers naturally had a problem with this Pauline idea of degrees of faith since they saw all saved persons as having the same saving faith. In fact, both Jesus and Paul regularly talk about little or large, small or great faith, and so it is no surprise that Paul would see this as something that should limit or guide the degree to which one exercises one's gift — one should do it in proportion to one's faith. Notice he does not say in proportion to one's abilities! This deserves further discussion.

With the professionalization of ministry, including the ministry of teaching and of doing scholarly work on the Bible, one of the tendencies has been to judge a person's fitness to teach purely on the basis of their knowledge or talent. Paul frankly would have found this tendency profoundly troubling. A person needs to grow up in the Christian faith, and indeed grow in faith, and as he or she does, that person is better able to rightly use the spiritual gifts

---

11. See discussion in Ben Witherington III and Darlene Hyatt, *The Letter to the Romans: A Socio-Rhetorical Commentary* (Grand Rapids: Eerdmans, 2004).

and knowledge God has given. I have known Christian people of enormous intelligence and with good teaching gifts who nonetheless were not mature Christians, who were not growing in faith and in largeness of soul. Paul would have had some issues with that person being given free rein, without accountability, to teach God's people as they want.

If the spiritual life of a Christian is vital, it is all the more vital for one who would be a Christian teacher or scholar of the Bible. This is one of the reasons James warns that not many of us should be teachers (James 3:1). It is an enormous responsibility to be tasked with leading people in the paths of righteousness as opposed to down the garden path. This need for Christian maturity and ongoing growth in faith is precisely why John Wesley said that the gifts of the Spirit should be normed by the fruit of the Spirit, by which he meant that love, joy, peace, patience, kindness, goodness, self-control, and other virtues should be the guiding qualities in a teacher's life and in how he or she exercises those gifts. A teacher or scholar should model Christlike character, not merely have brilliant intellect or present bold new ideas. If a teacher or scholar can't speak the truth in love, such a person is not yet ready to speak or teach it.

There is, in fact, a kind of principle of analogy that *is* found in the Bible, namely, the principle of typology. Typology involves the notion that there is a historical type and an antetype (e.g., Jesus and Melchizedek in Hebrews); the antetype foreshadows the type and indeed sets up an anticipation that there will be a greater and more fulfilling example of this sort of person later. The idea in this case has to do with God's operating in a similar fashion in various eras of salvation history, preparing for the climax of revelation in its earlier stages by prefigurements.

This whole notion presupposes the idea of progressive revelation. This is an idea that not only the author of Hebrews, but also Paul seems to operate with (cf. 1 Cor. 10, where the Exodus events are seen as analogous to some aspects of Corinthian experience and Christian teaching). More could be said along these lines, but we need to move on to the issue of how to move from interpretation to application of God's Word today.

The typological use of the OT in Hebrews and elsewhere reminds us once more that the earliest Christians thought that the OT speaks to Christians even in their new situation after the Christ-event. But how? I would suggest that we first must recognize: (1) we are not under the old covenant any more in any of its administrations, but (2) a good bit of the old covenant is renewed in the new, and (3) even in texts that are not ethically binding on Christians, if we but ask the right questions of the text, we can certainly find a late Word of God to preach or teach from that text to a Christian audience.

Rule Four: *Sensus Literalis* versus *Sensus Plenior*

This Latin distinction has to do with the difference between a literal sense of the text and its fuller sense, which is to say its deeper or even hidden meaning. This mode of interpreting the biblical text became common in the Middle Ages and led to allegorizing the text (especially the parables). Augustine's interpretation of the Good Samaritan parable is notorious. In it he claimed that the good Samaritan was Jesus, that he was administering the sacraments to the man lying on the side of the road who was dead in sin, that the church was the inn, with the innkeeper being the minister, and the coins paid penance money, and so on. All of this was justified on the basis of the principle of the "deeper sense" of the text. The problem, of course, was that this was not a deeper meaning that either Jesus could have encoded into this parable or his original audience could have understood him as promoting. There was no church or sacraments in that sense when Jesus taught this parable.

If, however, we ask the question whether an author can say more than he or she realizes, the answer must be—of course! In dealing with an inspired text one can argue that God was speaking at a deeper level than the human author fully realized at the time, as, for example, in a prophetic text like Isaiah 53. Did the human author of Isaiah 53 realize he was talking about Jesus, or even an individual messianic figure? Perhaps not. Some prophetic and poetic texts may have a fuller sense. If so, perhaps particularly with prophetic texts and the psalms being understood by the earliest Christians to have a fuller meaning, do we then look for fulfillment of the literal sense of those same texts, or only of its deeper sense, or both? Or, should we stick with the notion that a text may have a fuller significance later, not a fuller meaning?

Much depends on one's view of the roles of the human and divine authors. *Sensus plenior* thinking argues that when the text was originally written, God encoded a deeper sense or significance to it, which is different from giving the reader permission to "find" a meaning in the text. With *sensus plenior*, unlike reader-response readings, one can assume that there is a deeper meaning in the text, and so one does not need to creatively read one into the text.[12]

This whole sort of approach to interpretation has naturally made Protestant exegetes nervous because there seems to be no limits to what could claim was a "hidden" or "deeper" meaning in the text. There seems to be no controls. And when an example like Augustine's allegorizing of the text is pointed out, this makes such exegetes all the more skeptical about the idea. Better to stick to the notion that an author can say more than he realizes under inspiration, but it still has to be consistent with the literal sense of the text and has to be intelligible to its original audiences.

Rule Five: Prediction versus Fulfillment

Prediction is when a biblical author prophesies certain coming events. This may be distinguished from the concept of fulfillment. Christ is said in the NT to be the fulfillment of all sorts of ideas and institutions in the OT that were not predictive prophecy (e.g., the temple or the sacrificial system). Fulfillment, then, is a much larger category than prediction. Note the use of the psalms

---

12. Reader-response criticism is a form of creative reading of the biblical text based on a theory of meaning that does indeed suggest that since all readers are active readers, we are bound to, and indeed ought to, read things into the text. In short, meaning is largely in the eye of the beholder. Whatever else one says about this highly subjective theory of meaning, it does not accord with what the biblical authors thought about meaning. On these sorts of epistemological questions, see K. J. Vanhoozer, *Is There a Meaning in This Text?* (Grand Rapids: Zondervan, 1998). As the blurb for the book on Amazon says, "Vanhoozer defends the concept of the author and the possibility of literary knowledge.... He argues that there is a meaning in the text, that it can be known with relative adequacy, and that readers have a responsibility to do so by cultivating 'interpretive virtues.'"

in the NT, which are songs or prayers, not prophecies that speak of christological matters (cf. e.g., Mark 1:11).

Isaiah 40–55, which is poetic prophecy, and the psalms, which are not prophecies, are the two most used portions of Scripture in the NT. Only a few of the psalms can be said to be royal or messianic in their original settings, looking forward to an ideal king (e.g., Ps. 2). Nevertheless, many more of them are used in the NT to describe personal experiences, such as Jesus on the cross quoting the beginning of Psalm 22. Here we are actually dealing with the principle of analogy, namely, that a believer's experiences are parallel in various of the eras of salvation history. Thus, while the psalmist's words are about himself, they accurately describe the experience of Jesus as well.

Here are some of the questions I would suggest we ask of OT texts that are not binding on Christians: (1) What does the text tell us about God? (2) What does the text tell us about God's people? (3) What does the text tell us about the interaction between God and his people? These questions can be asked of any text, and much can be garnered and learned from the answers we discover. But there is one more way, an experiential way, that a text of Scripture will come to life, namely, when God uses it to speak to us more directly in a crisis situation. Let me give a personal example.

My wife was in the hospital in Durham England in 1979, and we were expecting our first child. We were thousands of miles from home in the United States, and apart from any close friends or family. Unfortunately my wife's blood pressure had gotten out of control, and the doctors had placed her in the hospital some three weeks before our child was due. The blood pressure kept rising, and finally the doctor said that Ann would need to be induced. This upset her no end, as we had gone through all the LaMaze classes. She did not want the baby drugged as it was coming into the world. I well remember being at the hospital with her, and we had been reading through some of the doom and gloom chapters of Ezekiel, particularly Ezekiel 36. Suddenly in the midst of a passage of dire warnings there were these words of reassurance: "And I will multiply your kindred, and I will keep you safe, and I will bring you home."

Of course those reassurances were meant for the exilic Jews in Babylon long before the twentieth century. But God used those words to reassure my wife and me, and I said to her: "Honey, I think the baby is on the way. We've gotten a word from on high." I went home that night and did not change out of my clothes but rather paced the floor. My neighbor, who had a car, knocked on my door at about 4:00 in the morning to collect me and was shocked to find me ready. He asked me how in the world I knew he was coming at that hour. I told him we had had a divine reminder to be ready. Sure enough, Christy Ann was on the way without Ann being induced and was born in the late morning of August 14, 1979. Turns out, God knows how to use his ancient Word to speak to us in our very different situations, and he applies the text more effectively and directly than we could possibly manage to do. We, however, need some guidelines and rules for using the text!

Rule Six: A Quadrilateral of Authorities?

One of the pressing questions for Protestants that arise from the principles cited above and from our personal experiences as well is this: What is the relationship of Scripture, reason, tradition, and experience? I would suggest that if and when we are talking about a subject on which the Bible directly teaches us something (matters theological, ethical, historical, or involving Christian praxis), there is a principle that must be stated about the interrelationship of these four things. We can say that reason, tradition, and experience can all be seen as windows into the Scripture or avenues out of the Scripture by which we may express the truth of Scripture, but in no case and on no occasion should reason, tradition, or experience be seen as a higher authority than Scripture by which Scripture could be trumped *on some issue that Scripture directly addresses* and about which it makes claims on God's people.

This further principle is really the only one involving these four things that does justice to the foundational principle of *sola scriptura*. Suggesting that reason, tradition, or experience has equal authority with the Bible in any matter, or even higher authority, is a recipe for trouble and for compromising some of the essential verities of the Word. This is not in any way to deny that reason is a good thing, or experience is a good thing, or tradition is a good thing, but they all must be "normed" by the Scriptures.

To elaborate, a person can have a genuine religious experience without that experience being a good one. That something is genuine and real does not in itself tell us its ethical or spiritual quality, or whether in the end it is good or bad for the person. Without the final objective norm of Scripture, it becomes difficult, if not impossible, to tell the difference between a heart-warming experience brought about by the Spirit and some sort of emotive "spiritual" experience that is neither edifying for the person in question or glorifying to God.

For example, not far from where I live is Shaker Village in Pleasant Hill, Kentucky. One of the founders of the sect, Mother Ann Lee, had experiences that led her to claim (and her disciples to claim about her), that she had *all* the perfections of God in her, in female form! This went far beyond what the Wesleys said about being perfected in love by God's holy presence, such that God's love could cast out all fear in the believer and leave just the living sense of God's loving presence. And it certainly went beyond what Paul claimed in Philippians about not having yet obtained a beatific state. Mother Ann Lee may have had real spiritual experiences, but when compared to what the Scriptures say about such experiences, she was probably rightly judged by most to have had experiences engendered by some spirit other than the Holy Spirit.

Similarly with traditions. There are many traditions in many churches, and many of them are good. But if they fail the litmus test of being consistent and coherent with Scripture and a legitimate extension of Scripture, they should not be made requirements. For example, some low church Protestant groups have long had a tradition of no sacraments at all, including no Christian baptism. But this is surely a direct violation of the command to baptize persons in the Great Commission in Matthew 28!

With reason too we must be careful. A person can be perfectly reasonable and logical but be thinking in too narrow and small a compass or circle of thought. For example, it was reasonable on the surface of things to suggest that Hebrews 6 had something to say about the issue of postbaptismal sins, a major issue in the early centuries of church history. But a more careful and detailed exegesis of this text has shown that the subject of this passage was not sins after baptism, but rather apostasy after conversion—a far bigger and graver matter!

On Moving from Interpretation to Application

Different kinds of literature function differently as they try to convey their message to an audience. Narratives accomplish this basically by "showing" what they want the audience to know about belief and behavior, whereas letters, laws, sermons, and prophecies (except for visionary prophecy) accomplish their tasks more by telling what they want or expect. Moreover, we have all these sorts of literature in the NT; generally speaking, fewer mistakes in application seem to be made with material that is obviously didactic and direct than with narrative. There are many considerations to reflect on.

Sometimes when application is the topic, the material of the NT is broken down into two categories—principles and practices. This sort of process of discernment or ferreting out of materials from the text is undertaken in recognition that the text was written at another time, in another language, and to other contexts than our own, that there are sufficient differences between then and now, between that culture and ours, and that in many cases it is not possible to apply the text directly without such a process. It has been rightly said that "the past is like a foreign country. They do things differently there."[13]

One of the questions that must be raised from the outset is: Is there any such thing as a biblical culture, or should we urge that the biblical patterns of belief and behavior be indigenized into any culture? Of course, some Christian groups have thought there was such a thing as a biblical culture. A good example of this is the Amish, who have chosen the German agrarian culture of the seventeenth and eighteenth centuries as somehow the epitome of what biblical culture amounts to and should look like. The problem, of

---

13. Leslie Poles Hartley, from the prologue to her book *The Go-Between* (New York: New York Review of Books Classics, repr. 2002).

course, is that when one freezes cultural expression like that, not only does the world pass the group in the fast lane as it continues to change, but Amish practices become glorious anachronisms, echoes of a bygone era that make the Bible look antique and of no real relevance to the world today.

Not surprisingly, most modern discussions on this issue have opted for the view that there is no particular biblical culture to be found on the earth today, nor is one required or enunciated by the Bible itself. Of course, it is true that when one requires certain kinds of patterns of belief and behavior across generations and centuries, some things are identical between Christians then and now, and other things are similar. All Christians have always believed that Jesus Christ is the crucified and risen Lord, and all Christians have always known that there was a high standard of ethical behavior and praxis required of them, which includes things like truth telling and loving one's neighbor on the one hand, and worshiping God and sharing fellowship on the other.

What is noticeable in discussions in the NT (e.g., in places like Acts 10 or 1 Cor. 9) is that the audiences are being told that there should be fewer barriers between ethnic groups of people. God is impartial, the God of all nations. All are one in Christ even though Jews don't cease to be Jewish and Gentiles don't cease to be Gentiles. But the implication is that there is a far wider realm of "things indifferent" (*adiaphora*) than there had been before the Christ event.

For example in regard to dress, Christians are not told how to dress in the NT except they are told to dress decently or modestly, in a manner that will not distract people as they are worshiping God (see 1 Tim. 2). Or in regard to food, in various places (cf. Mark 7:15–19; Acts 10) Christians are told that no food is unclean, though some eating venues, such as pagan temples, should be avoided. Or in regard to housing or modes of transportation, the NT does not mandate certain patterns. In fact, it does not mandate much about day-to-day life except that one's entire lifestyle should honor God and be a blessing and a help to others. Moreover, one should avoid sins, which destroy relationships with God or other human beings and damage one's self as well.

There is, however, an enormous freedom of choice about mundane things in the NT, and the *absence* of ritual purity rules and other sorts of practices that are ethnocentric and nurture ethnocentricity stands out in the NT compared to the OT. All of this is probably the natural outworking of a religion that was ardently evangelistic and universalistic in outlook and wanted to convert other ethnic groups to Christ, not to a particular form of cultural expression.

Because there are so many commonalities between the experiences of God's people in many different eras, we find that by analogy there is a relevance and a pointedness to many ancient texts when it comes to our lives. The principle of analogy especially comes into play as we read these texts. From a Christian point of view, God is the same God, human nature is the same, and God's solution to the human dilemma is the same today as it was in the time of the Bible. Sometimes this principle of analogy is stated in the form of preserving the principle of the original in some equivalent practice when one is dealing with an issue of praxis or polity.

Step by Step

As one moves from interpretation to application there are a series of careful steps one can take to ensure one is making an application that is consonant with the original text.

1. Understand as much as possible about the original historical setting and context of the text, remembering that the true meaning of the text must be something that the human author and/or God would have wanted to say to that original author and audience (e.g., in 1 Cor. 13, "when the completeness comes"). Failure to attend to this rule leads to numerous errors and especially to anachronistic misreadings of the NT.

2. Hear the Word as it is addressed to that original situation (the context of the original audience is crucial here).

3. Hear the Word as it addresses our situation (here again careful attention to context and the way the Bible can speak is crucial).

4. Apply the original meaning to new situations that are
   analogous and appropriate.[14]

Of course, it is never as easy as that little outline suggests. The
principle of analogy recognizes that no two cultural situations are
ever exactly alike, but one looks for enough continuity between
the two so that the original sense of the text can meaningfully be
applied today. For example, the household codes in Ephesians 6
and Colossians 3 reveal houses with slaves, but we do not have
such households today, so some of this material is not directly
applicable.

The basic rule of thumb is that while principles remain the
same, practices often and should change with the differing cultural situations (e.g., appropriate clothing in church will differ
culture to culture). But there are clearly various mandated practices in the NT such as baptism and the Lord's Supper; this in
turn means that the NT cannot be reduced to just a bunch of
principles. Indeed, narratives especially resist such reductionism.

Especially important to consider is how narratives function
normatively and with authority. Stories are not told in the NT
merely for entertainment. They are told to inform, inspire, and
motivate, and they have a pedagogical dimension. Sometimes the
implicit message is "go and do likewise" — for example, when we
hear about the evangelistic efforts of Peter or Paul. Sometimes the
implicit message is "go and do otherwise" — for example, when
we read the story of Judas betraying Jesus or the story of Ananias
and Sapphira in Acts 5. The question then becomes how to tell the
former sort of stories from the latter. My suggestion is to look for
positive repeated patterns in the text. For example, the summaries
in Acts 2:42–47 and 4:32–35 of how the early church worshiped
and fellowshiped reveal a positive repeated pattern. Or if there is
only one pattern (e.g., that Christian baptism was required for all
disciples; see Matt. 28:18–20), we can be reasonably sure that the
author wants to inculcate similar beliefs and practices in the audience. Repetition is the key clue.

---

14. I learned these principles under Gordon D. Fee. See his helpful summary of his teaching
on these things in *New Testament Exegesis* (3rd ed.; Louisville: Westminster John Knox,
2002), 17.

But what if we find varied patterns? For example, in some places in Acts we find people being baptized with water before they receive the Holy Spirit (see Acts 8, in the story of Samaria). In other places we see them receiving the Spirit before they are baptized (Acts 10, in the story of Cornelius and family). In still other places the two seem to be part of one event (Acts 8, in the Ethiopian eunuch). What should we conclude from this? Probably that there is no normative ordering principle being taught in these stories.

Narrative parables function similarly to other sorts of narratives in this regard, and there can be little doubt that certain principles of belief and behavior are being inculcated by the parables (see, e.g., Luke's interpretation in Luke 18:1: "Then Jesus told his disciples a parable to show them that they should always pray and not give up"). These parables are not just sermon illustrations; they are Jesus' public teaching meant to instruct his audiences on important kingdom matters, not only in regard to what God is up to, but also in regard to what they ought to be up to. It is true that parables often have unsavory characters in them, such as the thieves in the good Samaritan parable. Thus, we must exercise caution before we jump to the conclusion that Jesus wants us to go and be like this or that character in the story. Sometimes he wants just the opposite.

Just as there is no quick and easy way to become a Bible teacher or Bible scholar, there is also no quick shortcut or substitute for doing the hard work of exegesis before one gets to the point of application. But the interpretive task is no harder than the application of the text; indeed in many cases, it may be more difficult to figure out how to live out the text faithfully today, especially in an increasingly less Christian culture, than to understand the text in the first place.

Exegesis and More Exegesis

When I was in seminary, there was a standing joke about the word *exegesis*. It was claimed that these were the last two words of our Lord before his ascension. Of course the reason for such jokes is that it seemed like the word "exegesis" was a "red letter" word, a sacred term, because so many of our professors kept emphasizing the term over and over again. Such an emphasis has a long pedigree.

Just prior to his expulsion from Germany in 1935, Karl Barth had a chance to offer a formal farewell to his students as the Nazis moved to strengthen their grasp on the intellectual life of the country. He ended with these words: "So listen to my piece of advice: exegesis, exegesis, and yet more exegesis! Keep to the Word, to the Scripture that has been given us."[15] This is still the right advice, and perhaps the single most important key to making sure we do not misapply the text today. Application without exegesis is bound to lead to misapplied, however well-intentioned, Bible teaching. But exegesis without application falls short of the calling to holiness of life and behavior, which must accompany the need for right thinking and true believing.

Christian thinking and believing must be fleshed out in Christian living, or we are like barren trees with no fruit. Remember that what attracts a hungry world to a tree is its fruit, not its bark or leaves! Some Bible teachers and scholars are all bark and no fruit. Some are all leaves and no fruit. And some bear fruit in season and out of season. The life of the mind and the life of one's faith and soul must be kept in sync, in touch with each; they must be part of an integrated whole that makes up the life and witness of the Christian Bible teacher or scholar. You must have some personal depth if you want to make a profound impact on your students. In our next chapter we must talk about the practical skills required in order to be a good teacher of or lecturer on the Bible. Here first is a little meditation on personal depth.

---

15. Quoted in ibid., v.

SOMETHING DEEP INSIDE

Between living and dead
Between heart and head
Between flesh and blood
Between soul and spirit,
Something deep inside.

Between thought and action
Between image and reflection
Between act and being
Between sight and seeing,
Something deep inside.

Between silence and speech
Between grasp and reach
Between alone and lonely
Between singular and only,
Something deep inside.

Between begotten and made
Between art and artifice
Between lost and mislaid
Between offering and sacrifice,
Something deep inside.

Between parent and child
Between Father and Son
Between many and one
Between finished and done,
Something deep inside.

Between union and communion
Between friendship and family
Between sister and brother
Between One and the other,
Something deep inside.

Between loosed and bound
Between circular and round
Between labyrinth and maze
Between fog and haze,
Something deep inside.

Between Spirit and spirit
Between breath and life
Between time and eternity
Between image and identity,
Someone deep inside.

Between appearing and being
Between thought and meaning
Between revery and reverence
Between wholeness and holiness,
Worship deep inside.

BW III
Spring 2003

9

HONING YOUR RHETORIC:
THE ABILITY TO LECTURE AND TEACH

Some people do not have the gift of public communication. I recently saw an excellent movie called *Get Low*, starring Robert Duvall. Duvall plays a Tennessee hermit in the mid-1930s who is about as articulate as a stone. Yet he wants to tell his neighbors his own version of his own story before he dies! The movie climaxes with Duvall's painful attempt to publicly offer his confession and ask for forgiveness of those he had harmed in life. It is as painful to watch as it was apparently painful to do.

Learning Is Not Enough for Good Lecturing

Sadly, some Christian teachers ought not to be teachers, but because there are so few pure research professors in biblical studies or in any sort of Christian studies, these folks become teachers by default. Some of them can't lecture their way out of a paper bag. I had a teacher like this in college. The running joke was that the difference between this teacher and the textbook was that the textbook didn't mumble or stutter. As cruel as that joke may seem, it was an accurate assessment of this poor man's attempt to teach. He couldn't explain anything. He just kept quoting the textbook.

Tragically, too few Bible teachers or scholars have had any training in pedagogy, much less in Christian education. Furthermore, they have never even been taught the rudiments of good communication. In this chapter I will discuss both these issues. To begin with, there is a journal for those of us who do teach — *The Journal of Higher Education*. This journal is full of helps, good ideas, teaching techniques and tips, records of good and bad classroom experiences, and the like. I commend it to anyone who wants to learn to be a good teacher in any field, and all the more so if you want to teach the greatest piece of literature ever written—the Bible.

One of the lessons one gains from a journal such as this one is that the computer age has changed education drastically, and not entirely for the better. We now live in the generation of people who are primarily visual, not auditory learners. I used to be able to count on students listening and taking good notes, but today you often have to get out the cattle prod to get them to take notes. Usually they come into class, ask where you've posted your PowerPoints, and then stare at the professor without taking any notes. It can be depressing, but it is unwise to ignore the learning styles of this class of students.

In my case, this has led me to integrate into a class not merely PowerPoints but video clips from movies and other visually stimulating things. From time to time I use a device called an Elmo, which is an overhead camera projection system. Thus, for example, I can put one of my first-century coins in my hand, magnify it, and project it onto a large screen for all to see.

Enthusiasm Is the Sauce That Spices the Substance

Another part of being a good teacher is showing enthusiasm not just for your subject, but also for your students and their learning of the material. If ministers and teachers in training cannot get excited about the Bible and about teaching or preaching it, we are all in trouble. In fact, we can tell Sunday after Sunday we *are* in such trouble, as too many preachers have actually too little biblical content to preach. They have so boiled down the gospel that it comes across as insipid or trivial, not worth the time of good keen minds.

Of course, zeal needs to be as the Good Book says, "according to knowledge." There is no use in getting an audience all fired up about the wrong thing—about bad theology, bad ethics, bad praxis. There is a story told about Knute Rockne, a football coach famous for his halftime locker room speeches to the team. On this particular day his team was playing Illinois, and the stadium and locker rooms were all new. After a goalpost-rattling exhortation to his team, which was losing badly at halftime, Rockne concluded with the words, "Now men, let's run through those doors with power and enthusiasm and on to victory." The team rose as a single man running through the doors Rockne had pointed to and ran right into Illinois's brand new natatorium—the swimming pool!

Besides enthusiasm, you need to know your audience and to gauge your discourse to the level, or just above the level, of the audience's understanding. It takes some time to get to know them. The ideal is to tease the students' minds into active thought and to get them to stretch so that their reach extends further than their current grasp. They must realize their need for growth in knowledge and understanding of God's Word. Every class should present some challenge to the audience to go further, learn more, search more diligently, and study harder.

The Art of Persuasion

Rhetoric, whether ancient or modern, is the art of persuasion, and any teacher or preacher must be able not merely to inform, but to persuade. He or she needs to be able to argue a case, present the evidence, offer a logical series of statements, draw to a conclusion, appeal to the deeper emotions, and so on.

The beginning of such a process, oddly enough, involves knowing the character and limits of your own voice. I have a strong voice, and so I often have to tone it down. In fact, my wife is regularly telling me to hush in restaurants because she thinks everyone in the restaurant can hear me, and shouldn't! If you have a powerful voice, or what has been called "preacher voice," you must take that into account. What may sound like ordinary volume of speech to you may sound like yelling to your audience.

Now in some faith traditions, yelling is "bonafide." Indeed, the teacher or preacher is expected to yell at the audience, or else they feel like they haven't been properly preached to or exhorted. In other faith traditions, however, "yelling" is precisely what a preacher should not do, and the audience takes deep offense at what seems to them to be browbeating and demeaning ways of talking. You cannot please everyone with one style of preaching or teaching, and you must know your audience before you begin.

You also need to know about your voice's tendencies, and you may need to compensate for them. Some preachers and teachers speak barely above a whisper; while that may cause some people to pay more attention, it is usually frustrating and not good communication. Other teachers and preachers begin sentences well, but then their voice trails off and a large part of the audience cannot hear the end of sentences. This, too, is poor communication.

You may have a high-pitched voice. Especially if you are a woman teacher or preacher, this can be a problem because people may see you as being too shrill. A man with too high-pitched a voice who increases the volume of his speech can end up sounding like a canary—chirping. Remember the voice of Barney Fife in the old TV show *Andy Griffith*? It's a problem if your voice sounds comical but your message is in deadly earnest. Ideally, your voice and its tone or timbre need to comport with the subject matter. A joking tone of voice is hardly ever appropriate at a funeral, for example. But there is a place for some humor or levity in good teaching and normal preaching. The Bible is full of humor, including in the parables of Jesus.

We can learn much from Aristotle and his successors about being a good teacher. For one thing, every good lecturer needs to attend to the issues of *ethos, logos,* and *pathos*—by which I mean establishing rapport with the class at the outset, setting them at ease and being favorably disposed to listen, then giving them a coherent, logical, orderly presentation of the lecture material. You should lead up to a climax, where you do some application and appeal to their deeper emotions to make sure you drive your points home.

The issue of ethos is important in another regard as well; we will attend to that in the chapter below on character, but here it is important to say that the way you exercise your authority, the way you present your material, and the way you come across to the class (you can be an authority without seeming sternly authoritarian) are important if you want to persuade your students about something. After all, if you are a Christian teacher, the goal is not just education but conviction and transformation.

You must also carry yourself with a dignity that befits the seriousness and sacredness of your subject matter, without being a pompous so-and-so. In fact, if you establish an ethos in which you show that you are also a learner on a journey toward greater understanding, you will likely have a goodly number of eager fellow travelers.

Carpe Diem, Be Prepared

Teaching or preaching that is effective requires being at your best when the moment arrives. You must put aside personal traumas, individual anxieties, and other distractions and focus on the task at hand. It is, of course, appropriate to use personal illustrations of a suitable sort to help your audience better understand the Bible, but it is crucial to remember that *it should never be all about you*— your beliefs, your experiences, and so on. Teaching or preaching should focus on the Bible and be illustrated by reason, tradition, and experience. Your students will want you to be genuine and authentic and occasionally share what God has done in your life, but this should be the exception rather than the rule, lest narcissism take over.

The most important thing is a well-prepared lecture or sermon. All of us have suffered through rambling, disorganized discourses that could rightly be called examples of stream of unconsciousness. One of the things I have learned is that as your mind begins to lose some of its luster, it is more necessary, not less, to have good lecture notes, a good sermon text, and a good set of PowerPoints so that you can be kept on task and on target.

True, there are well-experienced scholars who can get up behind a lectern or pulpit and let a speech roll off the tip of their tongue in a beautiful, even eloquent manner, and in good time and good order as well. If you are not such a person, lecture notes and preaching notes are necessary to keep you within appropriate bounds.

When I was a young teacher, I did write out verbatim virtually everything I intended to say, and before computers, my wife would type up my lecture notes or my sermons. I couldn't have done it without her. As time has gone on, I have found less and less need for such notes in the classroom since I teach the same courses over and over again. Since I preach less frequently, I still bring a sermon manuscript into the pulpit with me.

It is difficult to keep up to date with any given biblical subject because "of making many books there is no end" (Eccl. 12:12). But it is important to keep fresh in any field you teach, and when I read new books on this or that subject, I need to produce new notes or PowerPoints to add to what I have been doing. Every scholar or Bible teacher, regardless of age, needs to keep learning, to keep their hand in the discipline. One of the joys of having doctoral students is that the teacher learns so much from the students.

Broadcasting Broadly

It is good to have a balance in attending professional academic meetings and giving papers, doing church and seminary guest preaching and teaching, and also doing public TV and DVD programs. After all, the Great Commission is still in the Bible, and it requires that we do more than just comfort or edify those already converted. This is one of the reasons why I have done a good deal of TV in my career on most of the major networks as well as agreeing to a myriad of radio and newspaper interviews.

TV and DVD work involves a different skill set. You have to be able to get to the point clearly and quickly. The media are looking for quotable quotes and clear speech, and you must accept in advance that you will be edited. I once flew all the way to New York to do a program for ABC. I was interviewed in a beautiful downtown church, and the interview went on for several hours. When the dust cleared, there was exactly one minute of my time in the show, and essentially all I was quoted as saying was "No!" Now that's what I call a short sound byte. On the bright side, I had a lovely conversation with Liz Vargas, and would be called on again since I was seen as cordial, not hard to interview, and reasonably articulate.

TV is an unforgiving medium. It's hard to overcome looking bad on TV, no matter how sincere and apt your message is. TV ministry is not for every scholar. The public media have little patience with those who won't respond to direct questions with straightforward answers. But the opportunity to share the gospel with millions is always an opportunity worth taking, and you just have to accept that sometimes you will be poorly edited, sometimes misrepresented, sometimes be made to look bad. But at other times you will hit a home run, God will be glorified and people in the audience will be edified.

Obviously, both good and bad things can happen on live radio as well. I remember doing an NPR broadcast some years ago when the Gnostic Gospels were all the rage. They were interviewing me and a female professor from Harvard. She was enamored with the *Gospel of Mary* and other Gnostic documents, and I was saying these documents are much too late to tell us anything about the historical Mary Magdalene. The Gnostic Gospels only tell us about a heretical sect in the late second through fourth centuries AD. The interviewer, it was clear to me, had already taken sides in the debate and was determined to make my views look "ecclesiastical" and hers look "scholarly and academic." I was repeatedly addressed as Reverend and she as Doctor or Professor. These are precisely the kinds of things you may have to accept from time to time in the service of the gospel. You cannot let personal hubris or vanity get in the way of doing your best. I take as my motto in such circumstances the words of St. Paul: "I have become all things to all people, so that by all means I might save some."

Preparatio Evangelici: On Being a G.P. In a PG World

The way the doctoral dissertation system works, you have to become a specialist in something even before you can become a general practitioner in biblical studies. Life is strange. It becomes even stranger when you realize that only about 10 percent of all people who teach the Bible end up solely or primarily teaching their area of doctoral specialization. Yes, that's right, only about 10 percent. Most Bible teachers, whether they teach in Christian schools, or in colleges, universities, or seminaries, find themselves teaching a wide array of subjects. Only colleges or seminaries with larger faculties can afford the luxury of hiring someone who, for example, teaches only the Synoptic Gospels.

If the end result of the long educational pilgrimage is that you will likely have to teach a wide variety of subjects, then it makes sense that along the way, you take enough course work, do enough study, read enough books, *in addition to what you must read for your dissertation*, so that you can be equipped to teach a wide variety of biblical subjects. For some who are preparing for a career as a Bible teacher or even a Bible scholar, this may come as something of a shock. Be a realist and prepare yourself to be a G.P. in biblical studies.

You need to know both the OT and the NT. You need to know intertestamental literature as well. You need to know the ancient Near East and the Greco-Roman world. There is a lot you must know to teach the Bible in its original contexts, and you should not begin your educational pilgrimage with the delusion that you can just concentrate on Paul or on the Pentateuch. If you do eventually get a paying job in biblical studies, you don't want to have to be racing around four weeks before classes start like a man in a fire drill, trying to prepare yourself for a course about which you know little or nothing. This makes for bad lectures and poor pedagogy. It is better to study the Bible broadly all along and to do the full array of biblical languages even if you only want to teach OT or NT.

The first full course teaching I ever did was: (1) in Wesleyan theology at Duke Divinity School, and (2) the basic required courses in Jesus and the Gospels and Paul and his Letters at High Point College (now High Point University). My doctoral dissertation had been in women and their roles in the Gospels and Acts. Schools have courses that need to be taught, and they seldom match up exactly with your doctoral specialty. The schools, not you, will likely determine what you teach. You need to be ready for most anything that has to do with the Bible.

This is all the more so if you are going to teach in a Christian high school or liberal arts college or at a major secular university. Only the larger Christian colleges and seminaries have room for specialists. The chances of finding a school that hires "research professors" these days is like the chances of finding the winning lotto ticket by accident while walking downtown in Lexington, Kentucky. The chances are slim and none, and Slim just left town.

I am a rarity in that I was pastoring and was content to be a pastor, when a seminary called me and hired me to teach the Bible in Ashland, Ohio. I did not apply for this job; it applied to me. The same thing happened when I came to Asbury Theological Seminary. I am not much help to those who put themselves out on the SBL "meat market" during the annual meeting in November, desperately hoping to get hired somewhere. I taught OT and NT, apologetics, Wesleyan history, theology, and polity at Ashland. At Asbury I have basically only taught NT, and it has given me considerably more time to write. In our last two chapters we will deal with the personal sacrifices involved in becoming a Bible teacher or a Bible scholar.

SETTLED

Thrill seekers and risk takers	Lawyers and Litigants
Pushing the envelope	Suing to get their way
Racing up the slope	Heedless of what they pay
Until they no longer coped	Until the judgment day
Settled.	Settled.
Mate seekers and date seekers	Sports stars and movie stars
Combing the internet	Shining in media's light
Deciding to hedge their bets	Getting their image right
Tired of not finding yet	Stylin' both day and night
Settled.	Settled.
Politicos and Pac Men	Teachers and preachers
Always testing the wind	Thinking they know it all
Always prepared to bend	Ignoring verity's call
Whatever it takes to win	Pushed up against the wall
Settled.	Settled.

Pastors and ministers
Envisioning great success
Placing themselves under stress
Never confront or confess
Settled.

Scholars and celebrities
Touting their latest books
Explaining how much it took
"Give it a second look"
Settled.

"Enter through the narrow gate;
for the gate is wide and the way
is broad that leads to destruction,
and there are many who enter
through it."

BW III
December 4, 2007

10

THE CHARACTER OF THE
BIBLICAL TEACHER OR SCHOLAR

One of the things ever present in my own mind's eye whenever I teach, preach, and write is the need to become what I admire. That is, ideally the person who exposits the Bible should have the sort of moral character it demands. Sometimes, of course, the teaching of Jesus and other biblical figures is so demanding that one feels like throwing up one's hands and saying with Paul, "Who is sufficient for such things?" In other words, one is humbled by the text itself and its rigorous ethical demands.

I am not merely referring to the sense of being overwhelmed by one's subject matter and one's own inadequate understanding, inadequate language skills, and the like. I am talking about being overwhelmed by the moral demands made of a normal disciple of Jesus—never mind a teacher, about whom James's warning stands sentinel at the door.

Discerning the Difference between a Good Teacher and a Teacher Who Is Good

Sometimes I must be honest and say, "I am probably not a good enough person to be doing what I am doing." I realize, of course, that I am a saved and forgiven person, but it seems clear enough to me that one needs also to be a very good person in order to be a good witness for Christ, much less a good teacher of the Bible. When Jesus was confronted by a young man who asked, "Good teacher, what must I do to inherit eternal life?" Jesus' immediate and surprising response in Mark was, "Why do you call me good?

No one is good—except God alone" (Mark 10:17–18). I often think: "If Jesus could say this of himself, how can I not also say this of myself?"

Does this lead me to throw up my hands and quit what God has called me to do? No, it simply spurs me on to continue to grow in Christ and in Christlikeness and to see myself as a work in progress, a journey toward better emulating Jesus. Growing in knowledge is not enough to be a good Bible teacher and scholar. You need also to be growing in grace and to be constantly aware of how far short you fall from being the teacher or scholar God wants you to be. I have met people who were intellectual giants and moral midgets. No teacher of the Bible should have that kind of discrepancy between their brainpower and their moral character.

I must also say that I do not see this sense of being overwhelmed, inadequate, or morally challenged by the biblical text as a bad thing. The Bible teacher or scholar doesn't need someone to invent humility pills; just taking in and taking seriously regular doses of the wisdom of the Bible is enough to humble any normal person. What is bad is what Jesus regularly complains about—hypocrisy, a failure to walk what you talk, to practice what you preach. And there is something even worse, namely, using the Bible as a tool to manipulate people to get what you want out of life, without having any compunction about doing so.

Character Counts

There is an excellent novel written by North Carolina author Clyde Edgerton entitled *The Bible Salesman*. Some of us may actually have had the experience of selling Bibles door to door, particularly if we grew up in the South. In this novel a bright, innocent, and naïve twenty-year-old Henry Dampier embarks on a career as an itinerant Bible salesman. On the road in rural North Carolina, Henry encounters car thief Preston Clearwater, who instantly recognizes Henry's personal qualities. Clearwater convinces Henry that he is an undercover FBI agent who steals stolen cars back from car thieves, and he offers Henry a job as his assistant. Thrilled at becoming a G-man, Henry sells his

Bibles in his off-hours, falls in love, and ultimately realizes that Clearwater isn't an FBI agent and that he, Henry, is guilty of criminal acts.

It is one thing to be naïve like Henry. It's another thing to use the Bible deliberately to get rich, to bamboozle people, or to pursue a life of crime. I remember the story of drug salesmen who carved out the middle of Gideon Bibles to put packets of dope in them so that no one would suspect or inspect the real contents when they were shipped across the U.S. border from Mexico. The point I am making is that the teacher or scholar of the Bible — and I would add the Bible salesman — must do everything in their power to mirror the character of the moral examples the Bible holds up for emulation. One has to have integrity and honesty to be a Bible teacher. It is not enough simply to know the Bible well or to be a brilliant teacher.

If it sounds as if I am suggesting that one has to be a genuine Christian or devout Jew to properly teach, preach, or write about the Bible, I am indeed suggesting that that should be the desideratum. If teaching is going to glorify God, edify the saints, and even educate, intrigue, and influence the lost, then, yes, that is what is most needed. It is true that some non-Christians can put Christians to shame with their biblical knowledge. If we are just talking about understanding biblical texts and ideas, it is indeed possible for a secular person to teach the Bible well at the level of information. But just as it is one thing to know the Bible, another to know the God of the Bible, it is also one thing to know the Bible and another thing to know the Bible is true, and God's Word.

The Bible is not just intended for information and education. It's not intended to be just a great piece of literature that merely intrigues or mildly inspires. It's intended for human transformation, and a teacher who cannot help an audience with the latter is handicapped. Indeed, a teacher who has not personally been transformed by the text cannot properly embody it, embrace it, model it, call for emulation of it, and the like. The Jewish or Christian teacher who is constantly coming to grips with the text will be constantly challenged to live it.

Esse Quam Videre—To Be Rather Than to Seem

There's hardly anything sadder than to run into a teacher of the Bible who does not believe the Bible and may even have a guilty conscience about making a living from teaching the Bible. I have known a few such folk, and they, perhaps above all Bible teachers, need our prayers. It is true, of course, that God can write straight with a crooked stick. We all know the story of God's using not only Balaam, but Balaam's donkey to convey the truth. But these examples are far from ideal. Jesus wanted disciples, not mere marionettes that he could manipulate to talk for him.

The warning that "not many of you (Christians) should presume to be teachers" could be further amplified if we are talking about people who are not even inclined to believe the Bible, or even worse are prepared to caricature, ridicule, and stereotype the Bible, or use it to pursue their own unbiblical agendas. We don't need Bible teachers like that, especially in a biblically illiterate culture already prone to dismiss the Bible as a relic of the past.

In a Jesus-haunted but biblically illiterate culture like ours, it is unfortunately possible for a person to masquerade as or pass oneself off as a Bible scholar, while not being one. A famous story is told about Albert Einstein making a lecture tour of major American universities in the first half of the twentieth century. In order to accomplish this, a limousine was hired with a chauffeur to drive Einstein around from place to place. There were many universities that wanted to hear about Einstein's theory of relativity, so the lecture tour was going to be a lengthy one. After Einstein had already lectured at eight universities, he was on the road to the ninth when his chauffeur said to him, "Mr. Einstein, I have now heard this lecture so many times, I believe that I could give it." A weary Einstein replied, "Excellent. We'll try that at the next university. I will be your accompanying chauffeur and you can be me. After all, this university has never seen a picture of me and won't be able to tell who's who."

Sure enough, Einstein, wearing the chauffeur's outfit and hat, and the chauffeur, dressed in a suit, went to this university. The chauffeur did a fine job of delivering the text of the lecture. Afterward, however, in a question-and-answer period, one bright young professor stood up, commended the lecturer on his lecture, and asked a complex question. The chauffeur immediately replied, "I can see you are a very brilliant professor, but I am surprised you would ask a question so simple that even my chauffeur could answer it." At this juncture he pointed to Einstein, and Einstein stepped forward and obliged.

The Inherent Need of Integrity

There is a different side to character that a Bible scholar needs to develop—virtues. For one thing a Bible teacher or scholar needs lots and lots of patience. Despite the fact that our culture suggests we can have everything quickly, getting at the meaning of ancient texts in their original contexts is, or can be, a slow process. Sometimes the outcomes of a detailed and intense study of the Bible in its culture can be disappointing. It's precisely when the text does not cough up the results you were expecting or wanting that you find out what sort of Bible teacher or scholar you actually are.

Are you mature enough to say that you don't know the meaning of this or that text, this or that word, this or that fact? Are you smart enough to suspend judgment on things that are murky or uncertain? Or are you like the preacher who wrote in his sermon notes: "Not sure about this point, pound the pulpit harder." Do you draw conclusions too quickly to support your own preconceived opinions about this or that subject? Do you know how to suspend your disbelief as well as suspend judgment when the evidence and circumstances warrant it?

Intellectual curiosity is a good thing, as well as being passionate about a subject matter, but these attributes are not the only prerequisites for being a good Bible teacher or Bible scholar. Are you passionate not merely about your subject matter, but also about the *truth* in that subject matter? Or do you have a tendency to whittle off or dismiss the hard edges, the problematic bits in the biblical text? Are you aware of your own personal biases and preferences? How well do you take account of them when reading a biblical text? Those who do not take account of their personal biases and agendas are much more likely to play that old game of "twist that text" until it fits. There is a difference between sound exegesis and exegetical gymnastics used to defend the implausible or impossible.

There are differences of opinion among scholars about whether being aloof and detached is a better way to read ancient texts without bias, or whether being profoundly interested and passionate about getting at the truth about a text better propels one toward the goal of understanding the Bible. In my view, as long as you can take into account your own predilections, the latter orientation is more likely to produce an accurate result, not least because the person actually cares about the outcome and is willing to go the extra mile to get to the bottom of things. I like the dictum of Johannes Bengel that John Wesley was prone to cite: "Apply the whole of yourself to the text; apply the whole of the text to yourself." This latter phrase brings us to my next crucial point.

Let the Text Interpret You

Let's suppose for a moment that what the author of Hebrews says about the oral proclamation of God's Word is also true of the Bible as a text:

> For the word of God is alive and active. Sharper than any double-edged sword, it penetrates even to dividing soul and spirit, joints and marrow; it judges the thoughts and attitudes of the heart. Nothing in all creation is hidden from God's sight. Everything is uncovered and laid bare before the eyes of him to whom we must give account. (Heb. 4:12–13)

Let's suppose too that for the open-hearted and open-minded person the Bible exegetes you, interprets you, lays bare the secrets of your heart, and reveals your real spiritual condition, your faith, or lack of it. Suppose, too, that you develop a living relationship with the Bible such that it interprets you while you interpret it, and indeed that is the way the text was intended to work, in symbiotic fashion. This means that you must approach the text with an open mind; more than that, the author of Hebrews is suggesting that the Bible is a sort of searchlight revealing your real character, even the secrets of your heart, showing you the things for which you must "give account."

This means that the Word of God is intended to have a moral effect on the interpreter, not merely informing them but transforming them, sanctifying their thoughts and lives. Herein lies some good news. The character you need in order to interpret the Bible faithfully is in part shaped and remolded progressively as you continuously engage with that Bible, by means of the Spirit using the Word to accomplish such an aim. This ought to mean that the further you go in studying, interpreting, and teaching the Bible in an open-hearted way, the more adequately you can reflect the character required of the disciple in that Bible. In other words, interpreting and teaching the Bible can make you a better person. When faith seeks understanding, as Anselm urged, faith is strengthened by that biblical understanding, and Christian character is further developed in the process.

Justification by Doubt?

Another aspect of Christian character that is needed to be a good and godly Bible teacher and scholar is a willingness to give the text the benefit of the doubt before leaping to the conclusion that the text is: (1) riddled with contradictions, (2) is unclear, or (3) is hopelessly antiquarian and thus obsolete and irrelevant. One of things that has often surprised me about some Bible scholars is that they will not give the Bible the same benefit of the doubt they will give their colleagues' theories, even if a theory is wild and wooly. This I find exceedingly odd. Why should a modern writer be given so much more benefit of the doubt than an ancient one? I see no rational reason for this, but it reflects a phenomenon I have come to call justification by doubt, as if doubting something proves one is a critical thinker and therefore a good scholar of the Bible.

Bible scholars are a strange lot. I ought to know—I'm one of them. Some are eccentric, some are eclectic, some are extraordinary. But when you participate in the rarified air of biblical scholarship, a particular sort of historical scholarship, it seems that this discipline especially brings the peculiar out of the woodwork. Biblical scholarship becomes a ripe field where the odd try to get even. Perhaps this is to be expected since the Bible is Western culture's number-one all-time bestseller and its number-one artifact and icon, and a lot of people have issues with what the Bible says.

"Justification by doubt" is a particular trait of some biblical scholars — indeed, many of them, because it drives too much of what passes for critical biblical scholarship. A scholar tries to demonstrate his or her scholarly acumen by showing not merely great learning, but how much he or she can explain away, dismiss, or discredit. This activity in itself is sometimes mistakenly called "critical scholarship," apparently in contradistinction to uncritical or precritical scholarship. And having once trotted out this label, it is then assumed that any real scholar will want to be a skeptic so they can be revered as a "critical scholar."

Here is where I call the bluff of those who think this way. I was recently reading a fine manuscript by a friend and fellow New Testament scholar Craig Evans. He writes that sometimes skepticism is mistaken for critical thinking. Some scholars think the more skeptical they are, the more scholarly they are. Evans adds that adopting an unwarranted and unreasonably skeptical posture is no more justified when it comes to the Bible than adopting a gullible one and accepting anything and everything that comes down the pike masquerading as real scholarship.

Craig is so right about this. The Bible has survived the critical scrutiny of many of the greatest minds that ever existed over at least two millennia. We should not think that it is now in danger of being explained away, set aside, or shown to be irrelevant. As Jerome once put it: "Defend the Bible? It needs about as much defense as a lion!"

My main point is this. Skepticism is itself a faith posture, a presupposition that affects and infects how one reads biblical texts, just as ardent faith is a faith posture. It is necessary for any historical scholar to recognize and take into account what his or her faith posture or predispositions are as one approaches the biblical text. But here's the rub. Some scholars, mistaking skepticism for critical thinking, assume that they are being "objective," approaching the text in a value-free way with no axes to grind, while persons of "faith" are approaching the text in a "subjective" manner that is tendentious and predetermines the outcome of the interpretation of the biblical text. This is not necessarily true on either side of the equation.

There is, in fact, no purely objective, value-free scholarship. It is just that some do a better job of admitting this and owning up to their presuppositions and inclinations. I dare say that those who are aware of their own commitments and take them into account *and even correct them* are those who really ought to be called critical scholars, whether they are persons of no apparent faith, agnostic, or of ardent faith. A critical scholar is one who is capable of being self-critical and self-corrective, as well as being able to cast a discerning eye on the biblical text. A critical scholar is one who is honest about the text and about what they do and don't understand about the text.

It must also be said that it is not good scholarship to have as a beginning point a posture of distrust toward the subject of one's historical study. One ought to begin with a posture of trust when approaching any historical subject, not with a hermeneutic of suspicion. Proving, or even just showing a reasonably strong case for a positive viewpoint after you have assumed a strong negative only is virtually impossible. It's like trying to prove you didn't do something. Ancient texts deserve the same respect, benefit of the doubt, and willingness to trust and listen that biblical scholars want their colleagues to exhibit when evaluating their own modern works.

In sum, justification by doubt is not a good starting point for critical scholarship. You haven't explained something just because you think you have explained it away, any more than you have proved something just because you have demonstrated that the Bible claims this or that. Historical enquiry requires data to be carefully analyzed, not lightly dismissed or simply received. Skepticism is no more scholarly than gullibility. But both have one thing in common—they are both faith postures, not critical stances.[16] This brings us to a further point.

---

16. These last few paragraphs appear in a more attenuated form in an article I wrote for *Biblical Archaeology Review* several years ago entitled "Justification by Doubt."

"Let Go My Ego"

You must constantly remind yourself that you only know and understand an ancient text in part. Tell yourself that there could always be a further revelation through deeper study, or an archaeological discovery, or a number of other things that could clarify conundrums and apparent contradictions in the text. If you don't do this, you are in danger of becoming too enamored with your own point of view, too cocksure that you know better than anyone else what the text means.

Indeed, I have even run into scholars who are actually dogmatic about almost anything but traditional dogma. They are thoroughly convinced that they must be correct and that the Bible is wrong. They seem never to ask themselves the question: "Have you ever considered that you might be wrong about this, or at least badly mistaken?" That brings up perhaps a factor that is too little taken into account, and frankly has everything to do with the moral formation of the Bible teacher or scholar—namely, the human ego.

Perhaps the greatest obstacle that stands in the way of understanding an ancient text like the Bible can be the human ego. Human beings have an infinite capacity for self-justification, for rationalization, for preening, for pride—and this is all the more the case with intelligent or learned scholars, including Bible scholars. If you spend any time in the guild of biblical scholars, you will undoubtedly run across some for whom it is all about them, all about promoting themselves, all about gaining fame and a big reputation.

I remember vividly an SBL meeting where an older scholar interrupted a session in which one of his former doctoral students was giving a paper by walking up and down the aisles and handing out critiques and refutations of the paper! He had to be called to task by the chair for this sort of tacky and disrespectful behavior. There is something unseemly about a Bible teacher or Bible scholar whose dictum is, "I must increase, and he must decrease," who builds himself up by tearing other scholars down.

A scholar of Christian persuasion should be polite, respectful, kind, and self-controlled in the way he or she engages with other scholars, even the ones with whom they most strongly disagree. If it comes to a bad impasse, remind yourself that the New Testament counsels that we must love our enemies and pray for those who persecute us by means of character assassination and ad hominem arguments. I have experienced some of the latter myself on blog posts, and it's not a pretty sight. To be honest, sometimes I have not always wisely resisted the temptation to be overly critical of others with whom I strongly disagree.

Christian teachers and scholars must be better than our cultured despisers or tormentors if we desire to be a good and godly Bible teacher or scholar. We must not let a wounded ego goad us into uncharitable and unloving remarks and behavior. Sometimes this is difficult, especially if we are deeply hurt by something said or done, but such is the high calling of a real Bible teacher or scholar. Let it not be said of you at the end of your career that you had more to repent of than to be proud of in your career. Let it rather be said that you manifested the fruit of the Spirit in all you did and said.

Know Thyself

Here it is sufficient to say that Socrates was right—you need to know yourself. You need to know your own limits and possibilities, your own education, and you need to know what you still must learn if you are to be a good teacher, preacher, or writer without hubris and without compromise. In some ways, the opportunities you turn down in life will tell you as much about how you view yourself as the opportunities you take advantage of.

But herein lies a problem: your image of yourself may not really circumscribe who you truly are. We have all endured the unsightly spectacle of someone playing or singing in church who cannot really play or sing—and doesn't know it! But on the other end of the spectrum, there are those with too little a sense of their capacity, too low a self-esteem, too much fear of trying new things—that is, those who mistake self-deprecation for humility.

If Christ is the model of humility in the New Testament, humility has nothing to do with feelings of low self-worth. Rather, humility is the posture of strong persons who know exactly who they are, stepping down and self-sacrificially serving others. Too many students of the Bible with low self-esteem practice call forwarding—when God calls them to do something, they make excuses and say: "Here I am, Lord, take my brother." There is, I am sure you realize, a good biblical precedent for such buck passing: go back and review the story of Moses at the burning bush, and then remember that God would not take no for an answer!

The question you must constantly ask is this: What has God gifted, graced, and educated me to be? Am I a teacher, a preacher, a scholar of the Bible? Is this what God would have me strive to be? Do I really know myself well enough to tell what I am capable of? It is not enough to listen to your self-talk about this. You need to listen to the wisdom of others and the wisdom of the Word, and apply it to your own life. Then you will know if you are cut out to be a Bible teacher, scholar, or preacher. The sad truth is that too many of us, I fear, have settled for being less than the highest and best we can be.

It would seem obvious from this and all the previous chapters that there are many sacrifices one must make to be a Bible teacher or scholar. It's always a work in progress. In the final chapter, I wish to talk more about the personal sacrifices required. In some ways, they are the most daunting and difficult of all. But first a little reflection on Christian character.

ANTITHESES

Overweening,	Unassuming
Overbearing,	Always daring
Just pretending	Quite authentic
Never caring	Always caring
Brash talk	Careful talk
Trash talk	Prayerful talk
Cheap thrills	Real deal
No frills	Helping heal
Pure bravado	Love in action
So staccato	Gaining traction
Living Large	Full of grace
Not in charge–	The Master's pace—
LOUD WEAKNESS!	Quiet strength

BW III
December 7, 2007

11

COUNTING THE COST:
SURVEYING THE SACRIFICES

By this time you have probably realized the considerable cost of becoming a biblical scholar, and I am by no means merely referring to the financial cost. I can tell you that on the financial front, the approximately five thousand books I have collected over thirty years to do my work has cost me about $100,000. This is partly because I started in the parish—in fact, in two different parishes—and there were no theological libraries near me, and no Internet either. Today, things are easier, and it is a good thing to see libraries digitalizing their journal holdings and various other resources. You don't go into teaching or writing in biblical studies to make money. I could have made a good deal more money if I had stayed in the parish. Much more important than the financial sacrifice, however, is the human sacrifice involved.

The Sacrifices of a Spouse

A wise sage once said that before you put your hand to the plow, you should count the cost, or before you take up your cross and follow Jesus, you need to consider the sacrifices involved. My wife, God bless her, knew something of what she was getting into early on. I met her while I was in seminary, and she knew at the least I would be a minister, and that I might be a scholar as well. She knew before we got married that I was going overseas to do doctoral work. In fact, she gave up her high school teaching career to marry me and go to Durham, England.

I am not the one who has made the most sacrifices in order to become a biblical scholar; it is Ann, my wife. It was Ann who gave me $5,000 so I could buy the books I needed to start doing my doctoral work in Durham, and in 1977 that was a lot of money. People used to call us during my seminary days "Little Orphan Annie and Daddy No Bucks."

It was Ann who had never lived outside of Massachusetts—indeed, who had never lived more than about two hours from her home in Massachusetts—and who packed up and went with this vagabond to Durham. On the first night when we were lying in bed in Shincliffe Hall with the wind howling and the sixteenth-century windows rattling (and discovering that a double room meant, not two rooms, but a room with a double bed), Ann lay there and cried, being so far from home and all that she knew.

It was Ann who typed my thesis thrice over. It was Ann who bore us our first child in Dryburn hospital—Christy Ann Witherington. It is Ann who moved with me back to rural North Carolina so I could finish my dissertation and pastor four churches. I could go on and on about her sacrifices. Mine have been small in comparison. It is only in the last ten or so years that she has gone back to fulltime teaching of her beloved biology and environmental science classes at Asbury University. I could not have done it without her—no way, José.

The Sacrifices of a Family

Furthermore, someone who feels called to a worldwide ministry of Bible teaching and preaching must accept the toll it takes on one's family. In my case, it meant that Ann was the parent at home far more often than I was. While I did not neglect my family and I love my children very much, I do wonder what life would have been like if I had been able to spend more time with my kids.

Working for Ashland Seminary I had to travel to four different campuses to teach—in Detroit, Cleveland, Columbus, and Ashland. It was the Brethren that made me fulfill my destiny as a Methodist circuit rider. And it was difficult teaching twelve courses on the quarter system—twelve separate preparations—when I began full-time teaching at Ashland in 1984. I look back at that now and say—wow. I couldn't do that now. I was fortunate to get the three women books and one Jesus book published during those eleven years.

When I think of all the sacrifices made so that I could be a Bible scholar and teacher—sacrifices by my parents, my immediate family, my friends at AFTE (A Foundation for Theological Education), my mentors and teachers, my ministers and congregations—I realize that I was and am anything but a "self-made" man. There is no such person anywhere, anytime, of course. I owe my Christian parents a lot, not the least of which is their raising me in a Christian family.

But I especially realize that I stand on a lot of shoulders, and I was being propped up, prayed for, enabled, pushed, supported, encouraged, and loved by many people. Otherwise, I could never have done what I have done. I have many friends and a good family. I am a blessed person, and the older I get, the more I realize it, and the larger the debt of gratitude I feel.

Above all, were it not for the Lord Jesus who called me, gifted me, equipped me, and stood by me during dark days, I would not be writing this now. I feel I am surrounded by a great cloud of witnesses. Most of all, I am running a race following Jesus, the trailblazer and finisher of faith. I still have miles to go before I sleep. I still pray the prayer John Wesley prayed in his later years: "Lord, don't let me live to be useless." But even if it all ended today, I hope that I would hear the voice of Jesus say, "Well done, good and faithful servant, inherit the kingdom." But there are other costs to talk about as well.

Counting the Cost

You may think that the sacrifices I just mentioned are too extreme for you. You may be saying, "Jesus would never ask that much of me; I must put my family first." Actually, it's not true that Jesus wouldn't ask this of you; frankly, a disciple of Christ must put Jesus and his call on your life first, not second. Perhaps you remember the biblical story of what Peter said after Jesus told the rich young ruler to sell everything, give to the poor, and come, follow him, Peter exclaimed, "We have left everything and followed you!"

"Truly I tell you," Jesus replied, "no one who has left home or brothers or sisters or mother or father or children or fields for me and the gospel will fail to receive a hundred times as much in this present age: homes, brothers, sisters, mothers, children and fields—along with persecutions—and in the age to come eternal life" (Mark 10:28–30).

Jesus wasn't kidding when he warned the cost of following him was high. Jesus had called his disciples to be: *mathētai*, "learners" or "disciples." Jesus himself was a teacher, and he called those who followed him to come and learn of, about, and from him. It was an on-the-job educational process. It is unlikely that he would not make some stringent demands of you in regard to your education and training to be a Christian teacher or scholar. John Wesley in his Covenanting Service put it this way.

In so giving yourselves to the Lord, you affirm that you will be heartily contented that He assign you to your work. Let Him assign you to your work. Christ has many services to be done; some are more easy and honorable, others more difficult and menial. Some are suitable to our inclinations and interests; others are contrary to both. In some we may please Christ and please ourselves, as when He requires us to feed and clothe ourselves. Indeed, there are some spiritual duties that are more pleasing than others; as to rejoice in the Lord, to bless and praise God. These are the sweet works of a Christian. But then there are other works. In these we cannot please Christ except by denying ourselves, as in enduring the sins and shortcomings of others, reproving others for their sins, withdrawing from their company; as in witnessing against their wickedness. Confessing Christ and His name is never easy when it costs us shame and ridicule. It is never easy to sail against the wind, swim against the tide, surrender our rights and privileges because Jesus Christ is our Lord. See what it is that Christ expects and then yield yourselves to His whole will. Do not think of making your own terms with Christ; that will never be allowed. Let us now approach Christ in prayer.

I have tried hard to live my life by the teachings of Jesus, and by such guidance as Mr. Wesley gave me in this exhortation. It has not been easy, but it has been a blessed sacrifice. Not a sacrifice of the intellect, mind you. Rather, it has required a sanctification of the intellect and the whole self, and it's still a work in progress.

Yes, it has involved a lot of time, a lot of late hours, a lot of bone-wearying travel, a lot of pondering and poring over tomes and wrestling with languages, and a lot of personal sacrifices. I will mention but one. When I entered UNC Chapel Hill, I was a violinist. I was good enough to make second chair in the UNC Chamber Orchestra as a freshman. I love music, grew up on the piano bench, and at one point thought seriously about being a musician.

But I realized in 1970 that I would have to fish or cut bait when it came to the violin. It requires four to five hours a day of practice to be topnotch at the violin, and I refused to play it poorly. But when Christ called me in college to pursue the study of his Word, I soon realized that while I would not have to give up music, I would have to give up any dream of being a professional musician. This is what Jesus asked of me, and I did it.

It was a hard sacrifice. Next to Jesus and family and friends, I loved music best, until I ran into serious study of the Bible. In a sense, Jesus required of me to give up my first love when it came to a profession or vocation, in order that I might have a better one. So in 1970 I put down my violin and have almost never picked it up since. I put my hand to the plow on which was engraved the words "the Bible," but have not looked back in anger or in longing. Yes, there has been some sadness and wondering what I would have become if I had continued in music, but I have no regrets. The worth of the Word has made the work in the Word worthwhile.

Hopefully this book has encouraged you to pursue your calling, but without any illusions that it will be easy. I am well aware that Americans tend to become consumed with their work and become what they do. Too often when I have asked some high-powered professional in America, "And who are you?" the response has come, "I am a doctor (or a lawyer, or a teacher)." I am, of course, more than I do, but what I do matters. We were all re-created in

Christ to do good works. In my case, I was re-created in Christ to teach and preach and write. If any part of this is also your calling, it would be well to close this study with a meditation on a Christian perspective on work. My career of writing began with poetry. I intend to end it that way as well. Here is a poem I have written in recent times.

OPUS MAGNUM

Weary, worn, welts on hand
Work has whittled down the man
To the bare necessities
Of what he is, and what he'll be
Was this then his destiny?

Defined, refined by what we do,
The toilsome tasks are never through
Thorn and thistle, dirt and dust
Sweeping clean, removing rust
All to earn his upper crust?

Sweat of brow, and carried weight
Rose too early, slept too late
Slaving, striving dawn to dusk
Til the shell is barely husk
Staunch the stench with smell of musk?

But work is not the curse or cure
By which we're healed, or will endure
It will not save us in the end,
It is no foe, but rather friend
But while it molds us will we mend?

Task Master making all things new
Who makes the most of what we do,
Let our work an offering be
A timely gift from those set free
From earning our eternity.

When work is mission on the move
By those whose efforts serve to prove
That nothing's wasted in God's hands
When we respond to his commands
Then we shall hear him say "well done"
To those who worked under the Son.

BW III
October 4, 2005

APPENDIX 1:
PLANNING AHEAD—WHAT TO DO DURING GRADUATE SCHOOL

Sometimes I wish that I had had an admissions counselor at Gordon-Conwell Seminary when I entered there in 1974. Back then there weren't such people; moreover, there was very little wiggle room to adjust the courses you had to take to get your degree. But there was and is one fundamental decision that you have to make upon entering seminary or graduate school, namely, which degree program to be in. For example, do you want to get an M.A. in biblical studies or an M.Div.?

Even if you are certain before entering a graduate program that you want to do doctoral work in biblical studies, there are still a number of issues to weigh before deciding on one or another degree program. For example, I wanted to leave open the possibility that God might (and in fact did) lead me to pastor some churches at some point in my career, not just be a teacher for the rest of my life. Since my denomination requires an M.Div. for ordination as an elder and minister, for me the only choice was to get an M.Div. degree. Choosing the M.A. in biblical studies would have limited me to just a possible future in teaching.

Yet there was a price I had to pay for choosing to do an M.Div. I had to take classes in Christian education, counseling, and various practical ministry courses, which I was not thrilled doing. I would have liked to take more language and exegesis classes. As it was, I squeezed in about twelve exegesis and theology classes in three years. Still, I was unable to get in theological German and had to do that myself at Durham, sitting in on classes at the university while beginning my doctoral work.

One of the important things to say about graduate work, if you really are strongly led to be a teacher, is that you must learn all the biblical languages and take exegesis classes in both OT and NT to build a good foundation. Note that most teachers of the Bible do not simply teach in one testament; they have to teach both. For the eleven years I taught at Ashland Seminary in Ohio, I had to teach both OT and NT. Had I not had plenty of OT courses in seminary and had I not taken some OT courses while doing doctoral work, I would have been in trouble. To make a long story short, study the whole canon in college and seminary and take a variety of such courses at the doctoral level as well.

A doctoral degree in the U.K. is pretty much just a mentored dissertation, particularly after the first year. As a result, you need all the good classroom training you can get at the graduate level. In my case I audited and took detailed notes in a lot of classes at Durham University just to learn more. On further review, I admit it would have been good to take a class or two on pedagogy while in college or seminary, that is, a course on how to become an effective teacher. Too many Bible teachers have had no training in this area. In addition, do you know how to be a good speaker, a good communicator? A course in homiletics can help, or a good speech course that trains you in how to use your voice is extremely valuable; all ancient rhetoricians had such training.

Obviously, how well you do early in your graduate work will likely determine whether you will even be able to do a further degree. Furthermore, you will need a good score on the GRE, especially if you plan to get admitted to a doctoral program in North America. Good letters of recommendation from those recognized already by their peers to be good biblical scholars will help the doctoral program admission as well. Apply to a good number of doctoral programs to make sure you get into one.

I agree with those who say that if this long trek of education is what God wants for you, he will make a way, even when there seems to be no way. You should know, however, that doctoral programs are progressively downsizing in most schools, and scholarship money is becoming more and more scarce. You will need to do some good financial planning to do doctoral work in the Bible, and you will probably need student loans. Lots of sacrifices are required to do doctoral work.

One of the things that helped me get my doctoral thesis done sooner was the building of a good library, often of secondhand books. Early on I spent $5,000 on books, a huge sum for me in 1977, and Ann and I packed them into steamer trunks and shipped them to Durham in England. I was glad I did, and it was worth every penny. As it turned out, many books that I needed were not in the Durham library, and many others I could not check out of the library. It may surprise you, but in Europe there are some libraries where you can only use the books on site; you cannot check them out. So you need to build your own library, carefully. To that end, here is a list of twenty useful monographs for New Testamentlers that you might want to start with, and read them long before you get to the doctoral process:

Adolph Deissmann: *Light from the Ancient East*

Edwin Judge: *The First Christians in the Roman World*

Joachim Jeremias: *The Parables of Jesus*

E. P. Sanders: *Paul and Palestinian Judaism*

N. T. Wright: *Resurrection and the Son of God*

Richard Hays: *The Faith of Jesus Christ*

Ben Witherington: *The Christology of Jesus*

Anthony Thiselton: *The Two Horizons*

Gerd Theissen: *The Historical Jesus*

Richard Bauckham: *Jesus and the Eyewitnesses*

Gordon Fee: *God's Empowering Presence*

Raymond Brown: *The Death of the Messiah*

Craig Hill: *Hebrews and Hellenists*

Murray Harris: *Jesus as God*

Allen Culpepper: *Anatomy of the Fourth Gospel*

R. Tannehill: *The Narrative Unity of Luke-Acts*

Christopher Bryan: *Render unto Caesar*

Margaret Mitchell: *The Rhetoric of Reconciliation*

John Barclay: *The Obedience of Faith*

Ben Witherington: *New Testament Rhetoric*

You do not want to spend many hours on remedial studies when you get to the doctoral level: doing remedial reading and remedial language work, or learning how to write. Somewhere along the way during your master's program you should take a course or two in good professional writing, especially if writing is an onerous task for you.

Doing doctoral work will test your patience and, more importantly, build your character. You will learn a lot about yourself and how you handle stress and pressure. Having a child who is now going through the doctoral process in the University of Chicago, I am going through it again, vicariously, to some degree. Your metal will be tested. Of the thirteen doctoral students C. K. Barrett had when I was at Durham, less than half left the school with their desired degree.

If you were to ask me today whether it was worth it and whether would I do it over again, even in spite of all the obstacles and difficulties, my answer would be a resounding yes. There is nothing better in life than doing what God has called you to do. I have run into many people, many of them good Christians, who failed to do this when God called them to do it. They live with a lot of regret, a lot of second-guessing, and some of them with a lot of guilt. As the poet John Greenleaf Whittier (1807–1892) once said: "the saddest words of tongue or pen—what might have been, what might have been."

Robert Frost once wrote that you should take the path less travelled by, and it will make all the difference. There are few greater joys than having the privilege and honor of teaching God's Word.

I am thankful every day for this privilege. I suspect you will be too. If this little guide has helped you toward having your doctoral degree, I am content. May God bless you in your commitment to lifelong learning (and teaching) of the Bible.

APPENDIX 2: WESLEY'S SERIES
OF CLASSIC CHRISTIAN
WORKS FOR HIS PREACHERS

The Epistles of the Apostolical Fathers, St. Clement, St. Ignatius, St. Polycarp, The Martyrdoms of St. Ignatius and St. Polycarp

The Homilies of Macarius

An Extract of John Arndt's True Christianity, Part I

An Extract of John Arndt's True Christianity, Part II

The Second Book, Part I

The Second Book, Part II

The Third Book

The Fourth Book

Acts and Monuments of the Christian Martyrs Parts I-VI

Supplements to Mr. Foxe's Book of Martyrs by Samuel Clark Parts I-III Meditations and Vows. Divine and Moral by Bishop Hall

Heaven upon Earth, or True Peace of Mind

Letters on Several Occasions. Extracts from the Works of Rev. Robert Bolton B.D, Part I, Part II, Part, III, Part IV

Extracts from the Works of Rev. John Preston, D.D., His Life Extracts from the Works of Rev. John Preston, D.D., Part I. Of Faith Extracts from the Works of Rev. John Preston, D.D., Part II. Of Effectual Faith Extracts from the Works of Rev. John Preston, D.D., Part III. Of Love, The New Covenant or Saint's Portio

http://wesley.nnu.edu/john_wesley/christian_library/vol6/ CL6Part1.htm Extracts from the Works of the Rev. Richard Sibs, D.D. Part I Extracts from the Works of the Rev. Richard

Sibs, D.D. Part II Extracts from the Works of the Rev. Richard Sibs, D.D. Part III

Extracts from the Works of the Rev. Thomas Goodwin, D.D. Part I Extracts from the Works of the Rev. Thomas Goodwin, D.D. Part II Extracts from the Works of the Rev. Thomas Goodwin, Christ the Object and Support of Faith Extracts from the Works of the Rev. Thomas Goodwin, The Heart of Christ in Heaven Towards Sinners on Earth. In Three Parts

Extracts from the works of Thomas Goodwin D.D.

The Trial of a Christian's Growth

Extracts from the Works of William Dell

Extracts and Sermons from the Works of Thomas Manton D.D. Part I, Part II, Part III

Extracts from the Works of Mr. Isaac Ambrose. Directions to a Man in the Act of a New Birth. Extracts from the works of Isaac Ambrose of Duties in General, of Self Denial, of the Life of Faith, of Family Duties

Looking unto Jesus. The First Book, The Second Book, The Third Book, The Fourth Book, The Fifth Book, The Sixth Book. Looking unto Jesus in his Ascension, Session, and Mission of his Spirit. The Seventh Book. Looking unto Jesus in his Intercession. The Eighth Book Looking unto Jesus in his Second Coming. The Ninth Book.

Extracts from the Works of Jeremy Taylor D.D. Chapters I-III, On the Christian Religion. The Rules and Exercises of Holy Dying, Chapters I-V

http://wesley.nnu.edu/john_wesley/christian_library/vol8/CL8Part2.htm

Academia Celestis. The Life of Christ. The Pith and Kernel of All Religion

Extract from the Works of Nathaniel Culverwell

Extracts from the Works of John Owen D.D. The Nature, Power, Deceit, and Prevelency of the Remainders of Indwelling Sin in Believers. Part I. Of Temptation, the Nature and Power of it–Part II. Christologia, or a Declaration of the Glorious Mystery of the Person of Christ, God and Man. Part III Of Communion with God the Father, Son and Holy Ghost

Works of John Owen, D.D., Part I, Part II Works of John Owen, D.D., Part III Extracts from the Works of Mr. John Smith Extracts from the Works of Mr. John Smith: A Short Discourse on Atheism Extracts from the Works of Mr. John Smith: Concerning the Nature and Existence of God Extracts from the Works of Mr. John Smith: The Nature of Prophecy Extracts from the Works of Mr. John Smith: Treating Legal Righteousness Extracts from the Works of Mr. John Smith: Vanity of Pharisaic Righteousness, Part I Extracts from the Works of Mr. John Smith: Vanity of Pharisaic Righteousness, Part II Extracts from the Works of Mr. John Smith: Christian Conflicts and Conquests

Memorials of Godliness and Christianity. An Extract from the Whole Duty of Man, Part. I-III. Part IV-VIII,Part IX-XII. Private Devotions for Several Occasions. A Collection of Prayers for Families. Directions for Married Persons Chap. I-VIII, Chap. IX-XV.

Extracts from the Work of Bishop Sanderson, Part II.

A Discourse concerning Comparative Religion. Thoughts on Religion and other Subjects, Chap. XII-XXIV, Chap. XXV-XXX. The Great Duty of Self-Resignation to the Divine Will, Part I, Part II Chap. I-VIII, Chap. IX-XII.

Extracts from Bishop Ken

Extracts from the Works of Mr. Joseph Allein. An Alarm to Unconverted Sinners, Part I. An Alarm to Unconverted Sinners. Part II. A Counsel for Personal and Family Godliness.

Extracts from the Works of Mr. Samuel Shaw, Chap. I-IV, Chap. V-VII. Communion with God. A Sermon on the Final Judgment. The Assembly's Shorter Catechism.

The Lives of Various Eminent Persons, Chiefly Extracted from Mr. Samuel Clark.

The Lives of Galeacius Caracciolus and Bernard Gilpin. The Lives of William Whitaker, Phili De Morney, John Bruen, and Richard Blackerby. The Lives of Henry Alting, Fredrick Spanheim, Philip Sidney, Richard Mather and John Row.

The Lives of Joseph Woodward, Nicholas Leverton, Sir Nathanael Barnardiston, and Samuel Fairclough. The Lives of Richard Hooker, Sir Henry Wooton, Dr. Donne, and George Herbert

Life of Bishop Bedell Part I, Part II.

The Life of Archbishop Usher.

Letters of Mr. Samuel Rutherford Part I, Part II, Part III
The Works of Anthony Horneck. Exercise I-VI, Exercise VII-XV
The Lives of Primitive Christians

Works of Hugh Binning, Sermons I-III Works of Hugh Binning, Sermons IV-V Life of Matthew Hale Contemplations by Sir. Matthew Hale, Part I Contemplations by Sir. Matthew Hale, Part II Extracts from the Work of Simon Patrick: Extract from the Christian Sacrifice, Part I Extracts from the Work of Simon Patrick: Extract from the Christian Sacrifice, Part II Extracts from the Work of Simon Patrick: Extract from the Christian Sacrifice, Part III

Extracts from the works of Richard Allen–A Vindication of Godliness, Discourse I A Vindication of Godliness, Discourse II A Vindication of Godliness: The Application of the Whole, Part I A Vindication of Godliness: The Application of the Whole, Part II A Rebuke to Backsliders, Part I A Rebuke to Backsliders, Part II A Rebuke to Backsliders, Part III The Necessity of Godly Fear The Necessity of Godly Fear: The Application, Part I The Necessity of Godly Fear: The Application, Part II

Primitive Christianity, By Dr. Cave, Part I Primitive Christianity, By Dr. Cave, Part II Primitive Christianity, By Dr. Cave, Part III

A Relation of the Holy War, By John Bunyan, Part I A Relation of the Holy War, By John Bunyan, Part II A Gospel Glass, Part I A Gospel Glass, Part II A Gospel Glass, Part III A Gospel Glass, Part IV A Gospel Glass, Part V.

Extracts from Mr. Cowley's Essays. Extracts from Dr. Goodman's Evening Conference Part I, Sec. I. Extracts from Dr. Goodman's Evening Conference, Part I, Sec. II Extracts from Dr. Goodman's Evening Conference, Part II, Sec. I Extracts from Dr. Goodman's Evening Conference, Part II, Sec. II Extracts from Dr. Goodman's Evening Conference, Part III, Sec. I Extracts from Dr. Goodman's Evening Conference, Part III, Sec. II Works of Robert Leighton: Exposition of the Creed Works of Robert Leighton: Sermons I-IV Thoughts of Religion, by Bishop Beveridge, Articles I-VI Thoughts of Religion, by Bishop Beveridge, Articles VII-X Thoughts of Religion, by Bishop Beveridge, Resolutions, Part I Thoughts of Religion, by Bishop Beveridge, Resolutions, Part II

Sermons Extracted from Dr. Isaac Barrow – Sermons I-II, IV-VII, VIII-X

The Works of Rev. John Brown, Chapter I-VII, Chap. VII-XIX. Extract from a Treatise of Solid Virtue, Letters I-XII, Letters XIII-XXV. Sermon Preached at Crippelgate, by Rev. Mr. Kitchen and Rev. Matthew Pool.

The Saint's Everlasting Rest by Richard Baxter Part I, Part II Chap. I-XII. Part III, Chap. I-X

Extract from a Prospect of Divine Providence, Observation I-XXII

Letters to the Duke of Burgundy

From M. De Fenelon

Archbishop of Cambray

Devotional Tracts, Part I Devotional Tracts, Part II A Mother's Advice Molinos's Spiritual Guide, Part I Molinos's Spiritual Guide, Part II Extracts from the Sermons of Dr. Henry Moore, Discourse I-II Extracts from the Sermons of Dr. Henry Moore, Discourse III-V Extracts from the Works of Stephen Charnock, Discourse I Extracts from the Works of Stephen Charnock, Discourse II Extracts from the Sermons of Dr. Calamy Discourse of Important Subjects, By Henry Scougal: Sermons I-II Discourse of Important Subjects, By Henry Scougal: Sermons III-VI

Extracts from the Sermons of Dr. Annesley. An Inquiry after Happiness, Richard Lucase Part I, Sec. I-II Sec. III An Inquiry after Happiness, Richard Lucas, Part II, Sec. I-II An Inquiry after Happiness, Richard Lucas, Part II, Sec. III An Inquiry after Happiness, Richard Lucas, Part III, Sec. I An Inquiry after Happiness, Richard Lucas, Part III, Sec. II An Inquiry after Happiness, Richard Lucas, Part III, Sec. III A Sermon by Dr. Annesley Sermon I-VI. Devotions: Sunday through Tuesday; Devotions Wednesday through Thursday. Devotions Friday through Saturday. Devotions for the Great Festivals. The Office of the Saints Occasional Devotions

The Office of the Saints

Extracts from the Sermons of Dr. R. South—Sermons I-IX. Young's Sermons I-XIII. Howe's Extracts Juan D' Avila's Spiritual Letters. Parson's Advice Part I: Serious Exhortations, Part II: General Directions, How to Live a Holy Life.

The Works of Archbishop Tillotson. Extracts from the Works of Mr. Flavel, Chap. XVII-XXXII. Husbandry Spiritualized, or The Heavenly Use of Earthly Things, Part I, Chap. IX-XIX, Part II-III, A Discourse of the Causes and Cures of Mental Errors.

Extracts from the Lives of Sundry Eminent Persons Chap. I-XV

Life and works of Rev. John Howe The Living Temple, Part I The Living Temple, Part II, Sec. I The Living Temple, Part II, Sec. II The Living Temple, Part II, Sec. III Eminent Persons: Philip Henry, Part I Eminent Persons: Philip Henry, Part II Eminent Persons: George Trosse, Part I Eminent Persons: John Eliot

Extracts from the Lives of Sundry Eminent Persons Part I,II, III; Short Account of the Lives of Sundry Eminent Persons, Church of Scotland, De Renty. Christian Letters by Joseph Alleine Part I,II. A Short Exposition of the Ten Commandments, I-X. Nicodemus.

Reflections on Christian Prudence, Extracted from Mr. Norris. Reflections upon the Conduct of Human Life, by Mr. Norris. Concerning the Nature of Future Happiness The Present Revival of Religion, by John Edwards, Part I-II The Present Revival of Religion, by John Edwards, Part III-IV The Present Revival of Religion, by John Edwards, Part V The Present Revival of Religion, by John Edwards, Distinguished Marks Religious Reflections, by John Edwards, Part I-II Religious Reflections, by John Edwards, Part III-Conclusion

Share Your Thoughts

With the Author: Your comments will be forwarded to the author when you send them to *zauthor@zondervan.com*.

With Zondervan: Submit your review of this book by writing to *zreview@zondervan.com*.

Free Online Resources at
www.zondervan.com

Zondervan AuthorTracker: Be notified whenever your favorite authors publish new books, go on tour, or post an update about what's happening in their lives at www.zondervan.com/authortracker.

Daily Bible Verses and Devotions: Enrich your life with daily Bible verses or devotions that help you start every morning focused on God. Visit www.zondervan.com/newsletters.

Free Email Publications: Sign up for newsletters on Christian living, academic resources, church ministry, fiction, children's resources, and more. Visit www.zondervan.com/newsletters.

Zondervan Bible Search: Find and compare Bible passages in a variety of translations at www.zondervanbiblesearch.com.

Other Benefits: Register to receive online benefits like coupons and special offers, or to participate in research.

ZONDERVAN®

ZONDERVAN.com/
AUTHORTRACKER
follow your favorite authors